PLAN LEAD GROW

SYSTEMATIC APPROACHES TO SUCCESS

Dr. Guido Quelle

with articles by

Susanne Fiss-Quelle
Martin Gierse
Holger Kampshoff

Mandat Managementberatung GmbH
Emil-Figge-Strasse 80, D-44227 Dortmund

Phone: +49 231-9742-390
Fax: +49 231-9742-389

eMail: guido.quelle@mandat-group.com
Web: www.mandat-group.com

Publisher: Verlagshaus Monsenstein und Vannerdat OHG
Layout: Nadine Pütter
DTP-Support: Silke Budde, Nadine Karoline Müller

Source Cover: © mao-in-photo - Fotolia

The Deutsche Nationalbibliothek (German National Library) lists this publication
in the Deutsche Nationalbibliografie (German National Bibliography); detailed
bibliographic data are available in the Internet at http://dnb.d-nb.de.

ISBN 978-386582-970-2

EDITION OCTOPUS

About the Authors

Dr. Guido Quelle

is one of the rare people worldwide who focuses on creating profitable and sustainable growth as an entrepreneur, consultant, author and speaker for more than 20 years. His clients are active business executives, entrepreneurs and directors who are committed to consistent growth. Dr. Quelle is always in demand when individuals, companies, and organizations are seeking the support that will enable them to continue on a course of sustained profitable growth. With his consulting firm, Mandat GmbH of Dortmund, Germany, he successfully conducted more than 300 projects with 100+ renowned private and listed companies. His client list includes multinationals as well as medium-sized companies such as British-American Tobacco, Deutsche Post, European Dental Partners, Mercedes-Benz, Volkswagen, and Erasmus University at Rotterdam. More than 5,000 people were involved just in those projects that he himself managed.

Quelle is the author and co-author of more than sixty professional articles, five studies, some of them European, two university study guides, and three books. At the University for Logistics and Business Administration in Hamm, Quelle is a lecturer in self-management and leadership. His travels, consulting work, studies, speeches and lectures have so far taken Dr. Quelle to 20 countries. He lives in Dortmund, Germany, together with his wife and their two Leonberger dogs.

Holger Kampshoff

is one of just a small number of consultants in Germany who can boast a career from student assistant to general manager of a mid-sized consulting company – while originally having set out to become a teacher. Since joining Mandat in 1994, Holger Kampshoff has carried out nearly 100 projects for more than 40 major accounts, helping them achieve efficient processes, sustainable growth and resilient organizational structures. The focus of his work is on the reorganization of processes and the parallel or subsequent adjustment of the organization. Increasingly, this involves coaching senior executives. Kampshoff has discovered that significant potentials are not raised in the course of business processes as such but it is what happens in between that counts. Accordingly, Holger Kampshoff is able to help in particular those entrepreneurs and managers who are willing to question their traditional modes of operation and process structures, replacing them with future-oriented and growth-oriented structures.

Holger Kampshoff has written about the effective power of changing traditional processes and structures in dozens of professional articles. He is the author of the first long-term study on business processes in German trade companies, published in 2009 by Mandat.

Susanne Fiss-Quelle

has been a freelance facilitator and coach since 2000. She earned an excellent reputation as a freelance consultant by helping individuals, groups, and real teams become more successful. She always focuses her efforts on reinforcing existing strengths, whether of individuals or of working groups and teams. Whenever project teams need to be formed or existing competencies identified and characterized, Fiss-Quelle is in demand as an adviser, for successful companies as well as for non-profit organizations.

Martin Gierse

joined Mandat in 2005, having previously worked for BBDO-Consulting in Düsseldorf, Germany. Today he is glad to make the most of his experience not only in the development of concepts for his clients but also in the implementation of such concepts. He has already shown the value he provides in several dozen projects. Marketing and Sales form the red thread of Gierse's professional career. Therefore, the focus of Gierse's consulting activity is on the performance improvement of sales and marketing departments. It is at the interface between these two areas that Gierse raises major potentials. Gierse made use of his practical experience when acting as a project manager for the Mandat-study "Marketing & Sales – collaboration or co-existence?" (Marketing & Vertrieb – miteinander oder nebeneinander?). This study has met with great interest among the national expert audience.

Content

PART I

V

VI

For All Those Who are Not Above Striving
for Success Every Day

Preface
to the German Edition

This book was originally intended to be a compilation of the most important articles from Mandat-Newsletter from 2003 to 2008, especially from the "Know-how and Methodology" section. But as always, even in a supposedly simple project, it's better to be safe than sorry. After viewing and sorting through the articles, it became obvious that considerable editing was needed to make it appeal not only to those who contributed to it or who, as faithful readers of Mandat-Newsletter always wanted a collection, a "Best of" so to speak, but to the first-time readers of Mandat material as well.

So things ran their course and the result is what you see now – a newly revised collection of the best articles from the Mandat-Newsletter, restructured and enhanced by a number of tips and notes to encourage the reader to rethink his business and to critically consider his own methods and check out the need for innovations. The book can be read in sequence or selectively or used as a reference for more in-depth information on a certain subject, as even after revision, each chapter remains a selfcontained article.

With this book you can access the insights into the methodology and content of twenty years of practice at Mandat. A book like this cannot be realized without many helping hands. Special thanks to my management colleague Holger Kampshoff and my consultant colleague Martin Gierse, whose valuable articles contributed to the success. Double thanks to my wife Susanne – once as an author of the important management topic "conflict management" and again for her patience when I withdrew to my desk move the book another step forward.

Many thanks also to Silke Budde, Nadine Kunze, Nadine Müller, and Nadine Pütter, the assistants at Mandat who provided illustrative, instrumental, technical, administrative, and communicative support.

I would like to thank the readers of the Mandat-Newsletter for their extensive feedback and enthusiasm for the topics. Special thanks to our clients who give us their confidence for the success of our mutual venture and with whom we can continue to explore challenging new pathways. A fascinating journey...

Plan, lead, grow – may you find this book useful in all three phases on the way to success. If this book takes you a step further on your way to profitable growth, it will have fulfilled a major aspiration.

Dr. Guido Quelle
Dortmund, February 2009

Preface
to the English Edition

Shortly after the German edition of "Plan Lead Grow" was published, it became clear to us that an English version was needed, as the principles, methods, concepts, and experiences presented here don't know national boundaries.

Since the German edition contains some articles on practice that are relevant only to the German market, we replaced them with special chapters. This edition thus contains some articles that will presumably not be available to our almost 1,100 German readers until they will be published successively in the Mandat-Newsletter.

The very fact that there is an English edition of "Plan Lead Grow" is thanks in significant part to my coach and mentor Dr. Alan Weiss. Alan's entreaty "You must think bigger!" was – and still is – a considerable inducement for Mandat and for me personally. Thanks, Alan.

May reading this bring you many new ideas for the growth of your company or your organization. Implement them one by one.

Dr. Guido Quelle
Dortmund, September 2009

PART I

STRATEGY DEVELOPMENT & STRATEGY IMPLEMENTATION

Strategy is Not a One-Way Street
Errors in Reasoning and What is Needed

Strategy development and implementation is one of the major tasks of business management. Too often, the results fail to meet expectations. We at Mandat have been dealing with the feasibility and sustainability of business strategies for many years with both a practical and theoretical approach (cf. Quelle, Guido, "Instrumentelle Unterstützung der Entwicklung und Realisierung von Marktsegment-Strategien in Handelsunternehmen," Praxiswissen, Dortmund, 2004). It is crucial to note that most strategies do not fail in definition, but in implementation. This is where significant leverage is hidden.

Sphere of Activity – Business

Commercial enterprises in particular offer products and often services as well that are comparable to those of their competitors and they are thus increasingly faced with the need to position themselves strategically with their customers with a clearly recognizable marketing statement. Due also to the increasing complexity of internal processes and the specific environment as well as ever more rapidly changing external conditions, commercial enterprises have a significant need to systemize the development and subsequent implementation of their strategy.

There is a lack of suitable methods that enable them to support this process systematically on the one hand and on the other, to do so with a manageable effort.

Developing a new strategy requires systemic change management. But how does change management work in practice? According to consultants, three out of four strategic change projects still fail.

Errors in Reasoning

When dealing with organizational changes we have to realize the following:

o Problems are never objective and they are mostly not clearly defined.
o A problem rarely results of a single cause.
o To understand a situation, it is not enough to have a snapshot of the actual condition.
o Behavior is rarely predictable, and we cannot have "enough" information.
o Problem situations often enough get out of control.
o Even a good and effecitve decision-maker cannot enforce every solution in practice.

The Personality of Change Managers

Moreover, not only technical, methodology, or content factors are critical in determining whether a change in a company is successful or not. A change manager is needed, someone with personal integrity who – more or less a "superman" – combines the three components strategic competence, process competence, and an open, honest, trusting personality. In the end, it is his task to catalyze the proposed change in what is usually a complex, dynamically changing environment – and not on his own, but with the sustained participation of other personnel.

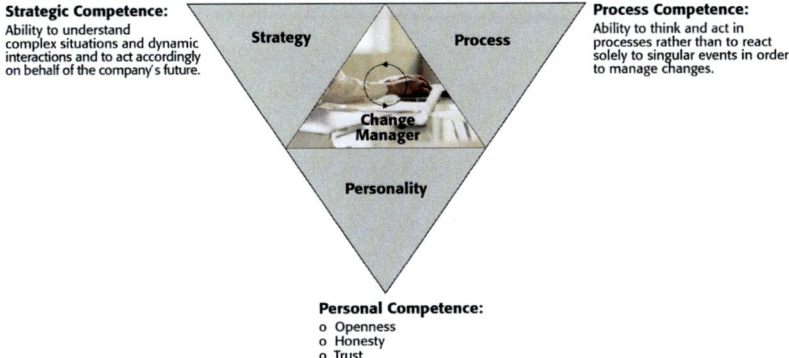

Strategic Competence:
Ability to understand complex situations and dynamic interactions and to act accordingly on behalf of the company's future.

Process Competence:
Ability to think and act in processes rather than to react solely to singular events in order to manage changes.

Strategy

Process

Change Manager

Personality

Personal Competence:
o Openness
o Honesty
o Trust

Figure 1:   Requirements for Successful Change Management

Requirements

Even if all the conditions for successful change management are ensured, this is only the sine qua non for actually implementing far-reaching changes. For sustainable change management, the following conditions are also necessary:

o   A formulated and practiced vision,
o   A clear, jointly supported and communicated strategy with unambiguous goals,
o   Common linking and binding values and work methods,
o   A pronounced, genuine culture of communication,
o   Uncompromising support from company management,
o   Balanced needs of the involved parties, and
o   Suitable instruments and resources.

Developing and implementing a (new) strategic approach is a considerable challenge for a company that can cause extensive changes on the part of the services offered, the performance process, or organization and requires professional change management.

The company management is faced with the task of having to trigger change in the own company while ensuring a process that makes the controlled autonomization of the change process possible so as to gain as many supporters for change as possible. In doing so, the necessity for competency in dealing with complex decision processes increases with the complexity of the company organization. A reliable methodology is indispensable for doing justice to this necessity.

While the success of the personality of the change manager can be perceived to only a limited extent, the previously described factors for the success of a strategy can be systematically and systemically supported by an appropriate framework. In the following chapter, a model is presented that enables us to systematize the tangible aspects of developing a market segment strategy and to support the methodical implementation of this strategy. It must be taken into consideration that it will be necessary to initiate and implement the entire process of developing a strategy parallel to the operational business if it is to meet entrepreneurial demands.

The 3-Level Model
an Effective Strategy Method

The fundamental concept of the method presented below is the following: there is a balancing act between a top-down and a bottom-up approach. On the one hand, the process of developing a market segment strategy is a management task and the needs of the company management must be taken into consideration from a strategic planning perspective, while on the other hand, employees must participate so that the strategy developed is implemented in operations with innovative ideas and expertise (and is not more or less offensively boycotted). The following illustrates the link between the strategic and operative concerns:

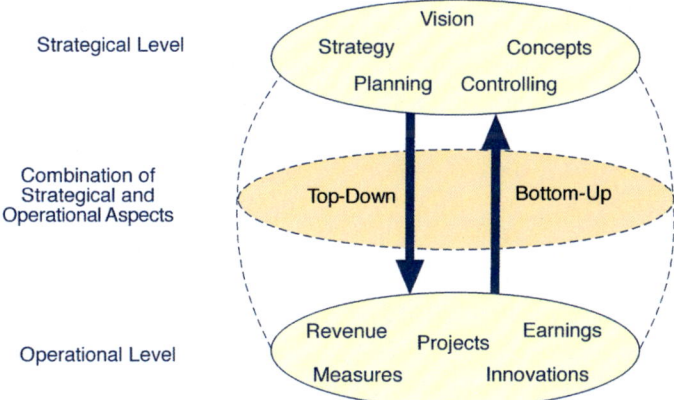

Figure 2:   Requirements for an Integrative Approach to Designing Market Segment Strategies

We can be justified for assuming that we must consider three levels in the development and then implementation of market segment strategies.

Level 1: Roots & Vision

At level 1, which we call "Roots and Vision," aspects are explored that shed light on where a company is coming from, why it acts today as it does, and where it wants to go in its commercial development and with regard to its role in society. This level is often ignored, which frequently leads to the loss of valuable opportunities to discover something about the "why" of existing behavior. If the "why" is not obvious, potentially long-term reasons for boycotting do not come to light. And vice versa, if a strategy team understands the reasons for a company's actions, which are often based in its past, it can develop approaches that acknowledge the past and still define a promising future.

Level 2: Development

At level 2, which we call "Development of a Market Segment Strategy," hard facts are sought, options developed, and decisions made. Beginning with the basic strategy ("Are we a price leader, performance leader, or innovation leader?"), which is often difficult enough to answer, economic goals that the company can and should achieve are developed by the strategy team on a well-founded basis and tested in the organization. But the crucial leverage is in the definition and conceptual configuration of the market segment. This includes observing the customers and their needs as well as defining the appropriate ready-to-use service offers. The question also arises here as to core competencies of the enterprise, the obstacles which the customers must now overcome in order to make use of the offer, and of course, the question of pricing every single service offer (based on the basic strategy). Questions as to competitors and determinations regarding the market and brand presence of the company complete the defining process in level 2.

The discussion is supplemented by an unambiguous definition of the systems and processes that are necessary to serve the market segment as competently as possible with respect to the positioning decided on.

Level 3: Operationalization

While the conceptual work in level 2 is already demanding enough, the reality test follows in level 3. We call this level "Operationalization of the Market Segment Strategy." At this level, suitable projects must be defined to translate the current status to the desired future status. It is obvious that this is a complex process; therefore it makes no sense to create projects at random. On the contrary, this would even be counterproductive, as unconnected actions have never benefited a company. Here it is necessary to define and structure the activities carefully, to appoint the right project manager, and find a method that is suitable to provide massive support for the process of implementing the strategy. For this, we developed the method of General Project Management, which has already proven its strength in numerous small businesses, beginning by eliminating every unnecessary project and in this way ensuring a striking start.

The Model

The three levels are illustrated in the following figure. It should be noted that there are cycles both within the levels and between them that make it possible to move from the strictly linear handling of the individual items dealt with in the levels to a method that allows corrections and refinements. For example, the case may arise where the vision must be refined a few times before work on the market segment strategy can be continued, or that the implementation yields results that lead to a situation in which corrections of the market segment strategy must be made.

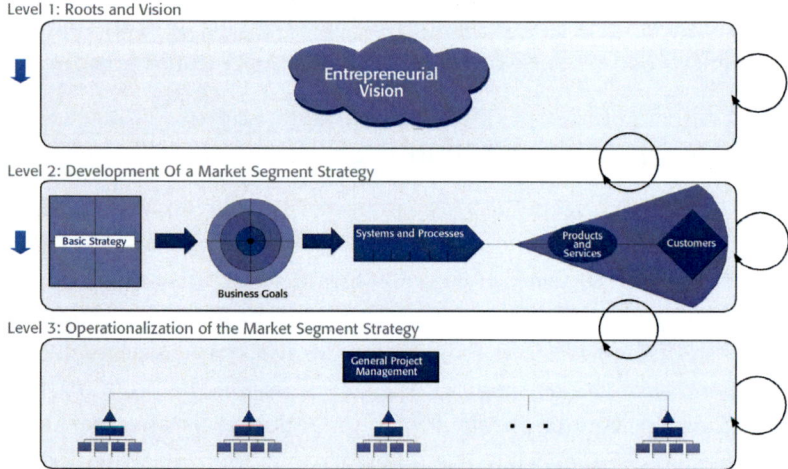

Figure 3:   The 3-Level Model for Developing and Implementing Market Segment Strategies

In this book, all levels and partial aspects of the 3-Level Model are illuminated in detail at various places. Where we are permitted to do so and do not reveal any confidential information, we have also included practical experience to make it apparent how practice-oriented the entire procedure is. After all, we always intend to improve our clients' conditions and this is the standard by which the success of a method must be measured.

Visionary Management
Does Every Visionary Need to See a Doctor?

"People who have visions should see a doctor"
(Helmut Schmidt, former German Chancellor)

We now enter the first level of the 3-Level Model – the entrepreneurial vision. Has any other element of company management been discussed more often and more thoroughly? Month-long consultancy projects and visions that no one understands – visionaries are simply "eccentrics." This view is often expressed and is supported by more or less reliable third party information. Especially in mid-sized businesses, the concept of vision is not well received and the development, enhancement, or merely taking note of an existing vision is dismissed as a superfluous, non value-creating activity. Results are what are required.

This is indeed regrettable, for especially in mid-sized businesses we often find very down-to-earth, visionary approaches, which however, are not generally described as a "vision." Is the word itself a problem? In any case, in our consultancy practice we often see that the actions of companies that have as clear an idea as possible of their future aims (vision!) are bolder and more targeted, that they attract the proper employees, serve customers better, fend off competition better, and earn more money than companies that simply wander at random here and there depending on current trends. Visionaries are not simply "eccentrics"; they are businessmen and managers who can imagine the future better than others. And good visionaries use this advantage systematically.

Requirements

The vision of a company is the basis for its entrepreneurial activity. By this we do not mean an arbitrary management idea that changes with the company's situation or environment. A vision describes a potentially never-attainable condition of a company. It may be dimensionless and must thus – in contrast to strategic goals – not necessarily include a timeframe. We can define a vision as a concrete image of the desired future of a company that helps the management to determine whether or not it makes sense to do certain strategical or operational things.

At a very basic level, the vision answers the question "Where are we heading?" as the basis for strategic work without needing to adhere strictly to facts. It does not need to strive for perfection – in fact, striving for the perfect vision can be counterproductive. And yet it is our experience that to inspire enthusiasm, the vision must set in writing, communicated regularly, and adjusted as appropriate. This applies to the communication with personnel as well as with customers, shareholders, and competition.

Dimension

The intensity of the activities to create and refine a vision is determined mainly by the phase of development at which a company finds itself. In the market development phase management efforts are shifted to the strategies and operative implementation of the vision. In the following phases of diversification, acquisition, and cooperation, the vision again gains ground in management's normative considerations.

In companies managed by the owners, the vision is more likely to be marked by the owner's personality, publicly traded companies tend to develop a vision, which, depending on the structural composition of the shareholders, possibly places a greater value on shareholder value aspects. At the end of the formulation process is the aspiration that the company claims as its own. This aspiration points toward the purpose of the company and ideally gives a first indication of the company's target group, for the purpose should be directed toward the target group. The strategy must serve the customer. The same applies to the vision

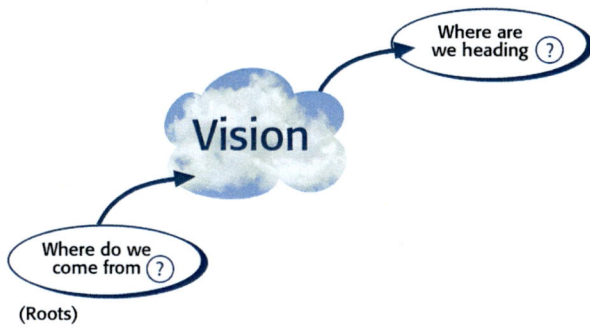

Figure 4:   Mediator Role of the Vision

Search for Core Competencies?
We Already Know What We Can Do Best
– Don't We?

The question of core competencies is actually quite simple: "What do we do best?" But – what exactly are core competencies? The debate on this has broken up many a meeting. The following definition has proven itself in our experience:

o   A capability of a company is a core competency if this capability
o   Can generally be influenced by the company and be developed by it,
o   Sets the company apart from its competitors well,
o   Refers to experience and know-how that enable the company to solve problems better than its competitors,
o   Can be used to offer customers significant value.

Why Search?

Admonishing voices – which interestingly enough are frequently the same voices that are heard stressing that developing a vision or strategy is just a waste of time – become louder on a regular basis to stress that the search for core competencies is an academically interesting activity, but one with no practical relevance, which takes up a great deal of time of all involved but does not ensure that progress is made. Of course we are of another opinion on this, as the knowledge of and especially, the agreement on the core competencies of a company are elementary for building on existing strengths, adding new ones, or even outsourcing things that do not correspond with the core. Core competencies are the foundation for providing services. They are fundamental in determining the success of a service offer. Protecting and adding to them is a lofty aim and freeing them from ballast is one of the main tasks of management.

Finding Competencies

At the start of the search, the creativity of an interdisciplinary working group plays an important role. Ask the following questions: "What are we particularly good at? In what areas are we objectively top?"

The result is usually a list of fifteen to thirty presumed core competencies, which must now be shortened. Are marketing competency, finance management competency, or IT management competency core competencies? No. At the most they are locations where concrete core competencies might be suspected and searched for. Consequently, in the first phase we distinguish between the content level (types of competency) and the structural level (locations of competency).

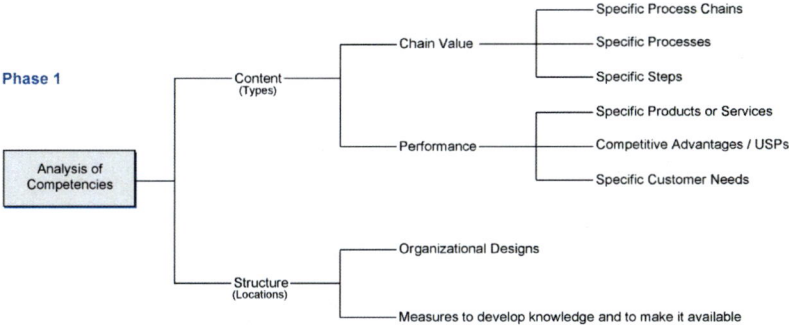

Figure 5: Analysis of Competencies

In the next step, relevant subjective and objective information on the contribution of the individual competencies to long-term customer value, to distinguishing from the competition, and to the existing potential for interchangeability in the future are importanF-

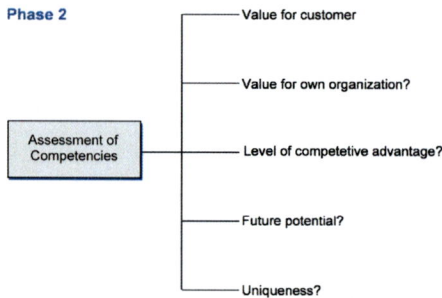

Figure 6:   Assessment of Competencies

Finally, for all remaining presumed core competencies, the issue of customer value must be addressed in detail. The following figure shows the issues to be addressed.

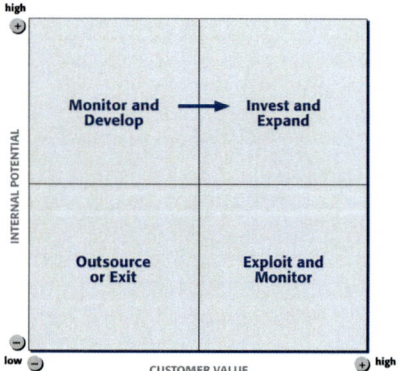

Figure 7:   Evaluation of Competencies

Generally, there are now four to a maximum of seven real core competencies remaining that have withstood all questions. These core competencies are now prioritized as to importance and the structuring aid has been useful, for there is a high probability that you now have identified and processed your real core competencies.

Personal Core Competencies

Everyone may be permitted to take a look at his personal development. The question "What are my special strengths?" is also significant when formulating personal goals. While the issue of core competency has attained a certain status despite all disputes over its meaning for developing entrepreneurial strategy, the issues and rules that form the basis for determining a company's core competencies are too rarely transferred to self management. This is unfortunate, as it can be assumed that every person has specific core competencies that distinguish him from other persons.

In order to formulate one's own, personal, specific core competencies in an analysis of the actual status, all personal strengths must first be gathered. In this, the question "What do I get praised for?" is an important indicator. In the first step, it is important only to collect as many presumed strengths as possible. The result is a list of ten to twenty presumed core competencies.

It can be assumed that a person, just as a company, has a maximum of four to seven real core competencies. In order to find these, some filtering is now necessary. In analogy with the company core competencies, each individual strength found is now examined with respect to the following familiar definition:

o   Can the skill be influenced and built on mainly by you?
o   Does the skill distinguish you clearly from other people?

o Is the skill related to experience and know-how that enable you to master certain situations and solve certain problems better than others?

o Is the skill one that cannot be copied by others easily?

o Can the skill be used to offer someone a considerable value (applies to professional as well as private setting)?

Decisive is: competency has to do with "can", not with "have". Generally, the loose collection of personal strengths thus yields, analogous to company competency four to seven real core competencies, which are usually formulated more precisely by experienced persons than by younger ones.

To make the list of core competencies as meaningful as possible, it is advisable to have previously formulated the strengths as concretely as possible. Generalizations such as "analyze", "deal with people", or "openness" should be made more concrete, for example "examine a company's performance based on the balance sheet" (instead of "analyze"), "lead project teams of up to twenty members" (instead of "deal with people"), or "start conversations with unknown persons quickly at conferences" (instead of "openness"). Such concrete formulations mark real strengths that make it possible to distinguish you from others.

The core competencies found are an essential clue to developing personal goals, for it is considerably more effective to strengthen existing strengths than to improve weaknesses.

I Have a Project, So I am Important
Half of Your Projects are Superfluous

How many ongoing projects does your company have? Three? Ten? Fifty? One hundred? You don't know the exact number? Then you are in good company. The number of active and sleeping projects is unknown in most companies and coordination of the project landscape rarely takes place. The reason – working on projects is important, has positive connotations, and the number of own projects is elementary for one's prestige. But experience shows that fifty percent – that's right, half – of the projects at your company are superfluous. They hinder the company's strategic development and your own personal development as well, as you may be dealing with items that do not seriously advance anyone. Resources are frequently wasted in an indescribable manner without any consequences.

Without a doubt – the implementation of strategic changes can be ensured only by dealing with the way projects are handled. But in addition, the issue of the systematic, consistent handling of several parallel projects competing for resources must be clarified.

High, Higher, Highest

Moreover, this raises the issue of setting priorities. How often have you heard in recent months that a project is given "highest priority" (or the rhetorical version pronounced with the proper fervor "ab-so-lute priority")? If the same project was always referred to, you have been lucky. If the pronouncements of priority have changed and you were involved in one of the projects referred to, you're out of luck. You have then slid into the priority dilemma. The result – decisions on resource issues and the sequence of items become more difficult. This becomes dramatic when the number of projects with highest (or just high) priority slowly but surely increases or if priorities are changed at random for no apparent reason. This is usually an indication of a lack of transparency in the company's project landscape. The relevance of this item can be seen in our study "Project Management in Commercial Enterprises," in which one question was directly at precisely this priority dilemma. It was shown that more than half of the projects in the companies participating were assigned "highest priority." A situation like this is difficult to manage.

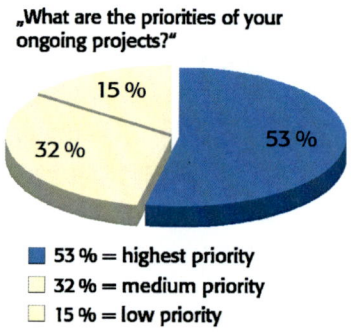

Figure 8:   Project Priorities [Mandat Study "Project Management in Commercial Enterprises", Dortmund, 2005]

If we are to take the concept of "highest" priority seriously, there may be only one project in a company that is given this level of priority. The departments are free to set priorities for their own internal projects as long as it is clear that at the departmental level there can be only one project given highest priority and that all projects must be subordinate to the priority levels of the company as a whole. Giving several projects at the same level highest priority is usually a sign of too little discussion of the items, indecisiveness, or simply a lack of interest and the misunderstanding of the catastrophic impact on the company associated with it.

Setting priorities is thus a basic prerequisite for clarity. Assigning priorities begins top-down; the company management cannot avoid this task. This generally involves actual hard work only at the start when it is necessary to impose some semblance of order on an existing project landscape and the large number of the projects it contains. Once order is created, integrating new projects based on self-imposed priority criteria is much easier.

General Project Management

But how can the management penetrate the complex tangle of projects and bring some light into dark corners? How can priorities be set in a directed and strategy-oriented manner and moreover, be communicated in a simple way? The Mandat method "General Project Management" (GPM) addresses precisely this issue. This method concentrates mainly on those change management projects that are indispensable for a company's success. In addition, the method is transferable to all projects of a company – even to those that are not directly relevant for the top management level.

When GPM is introduced, a company typically goes through two phases:

Phase 1: Structure of the Project Landscape

Phase 1 consists of compiling relevant data and information on ongoing and planned projects in dialogue with the respective (potential) project managers and clients. It ends with specifying key projects and the revision of the resulting project landscape by the management. Usually half of the ongoing so-called "projects" are dropped because it is determined that some projects are carried out in the same manner at different locations, other projects were created without authorization, and some projects quite simply do not make sense. In addition, there are projects that are still continued, although current developments have made the originally desired result of the project superfluous. Holding on to old habits is one of the biggest enemies of General Project Management. A good question to ask is about the reason for a project. Every client and every project manager who cannot immediately answer a question about the purpose must ask himself how important the project whose purpose he has difficulty formulating really is. The clearing of the project landscape in Phase 1 generally frees up considerable time and financial capacities. In addition, it often leads to transparency of the existing resource focus for the first time. Last but not least, the introduction of GPM leads to a considerable increase in alertness in the company and is frequently worth the effort for this reason alone.

Phase 2: Routine Operations

In phase 2, the ongoing observation and adjustment of the project landscape are ensured. The activities in phase 2 are concentrated on the aggregate reporting on key projects based on a uniform, unilateral project information sheet that is maintained conventionally in hard copy and can also be reproduced electronically on the company's intranet. In this way, the company becomes accustomed to dealing carefully with existing resources, concentrating on essentials, and competing for resources. Suddenly projects can be compared and their progress and results become visible to the inner circle. Of course, not everyone will appreciate this situation. But high performers will always be in favor of it.

Practice

A good example from our consulting practice is that of a wholesale business with branches throughout Germany that with our help built up General Project Management and implemented it systematically. After the first interview phase, 59 projects and undertakings were identified. The term undertaking is used for items that are described as "projects" in commercial language but whose purpose and objectives are so lacking in concreteness and transparency that they cannot really be considered projects. Even so, these undertakings usually take up a great deal of resources, which usually aggravates the lack of transparency and the damage caused by these items.

In cooperation with the board and after an intensive review of the purposes and objectives of the items, 29 projects and undertakings were deleted from the list. The responsible parties were informed either that their items were no longer relevant or they were charged with coordinating with colleagues to combine items with similar contents that were being handled at different locations in the company. The discovery was also made that in some strategically relevant divisions there were no projects at all and thus five new items were formed which were initially termed "undertakings."

It was then mutually agreed to remove the term "undertaking" from use and that an item had to be a project or it could not be assigned any resources. Due to the special situation of the company, half of the remaining items turned out to be extremely important and as a consequence, seventeen key projects were created. This was still a large number from our perspective but in this special case was due to the specific sector with numerous legal and content changes. Of the remaining eighteen normal projects, another ten were eliminated due to a lack of recognizable significance and in view of other priorities and two new projects were created.

Overall, thirty-nine projects and undertakings were terminated in this way and seven new projects were initiated. The bottom line was that the company was thus relieved of thirty-two projects, meaning a savings of more than ten man-years. These resources were deployed for a profit, as nearly all of the additional new projects enhanced sales, which had been suffering for years from a lack of concepts and strategies.

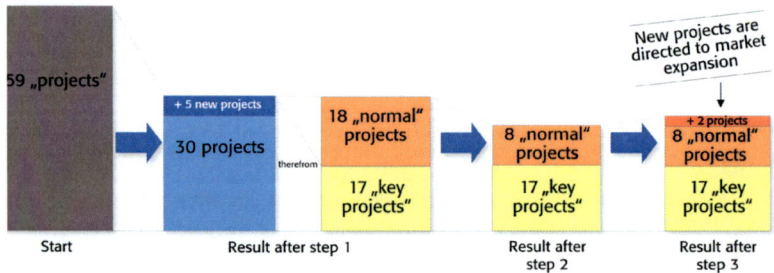

Figure 9:   Reducing Project Complexity

When is General Project Management Useful?

General Project Management is always recommended when a company's network of projects is no longer easily comprehensible. In addition, there are a few precise indicators that indicate the necessity for General Project Management. It is recommended when at least one of the following situations applies to a company:

o   There is no comprehensive information (from the management) on all already ongoing projects (lack of transparency).

o   The linkage of ongoing projects is not sufficiently known (to management) which bears the risk of doing things doubly.

o   Project priorities are not set decisively or are constantly being changed (chaos).

o   There is no cross-department, standardized procedure for projects (planning, execution, reporting, etc.) in the company (method egotism). One soft factor – the company management feels that there are too many projects.

Begin with Key Projects

For large companies in particular, the question arises as to where initiating General Project Management should begin, as it generally seems impossible to start with all projects or project-like activities at once. The question is easy to answer. It is necessary to use a top-down approach, to start with the most important projects, which we call key projects. These are a few strategically or operatively eminently important projects that the company management should be able to keep informed of regularly regarding progress, any bottlenecks that occur, and already achieved benefits. The following checklist is helpful in deciding which projects are actually key projects:

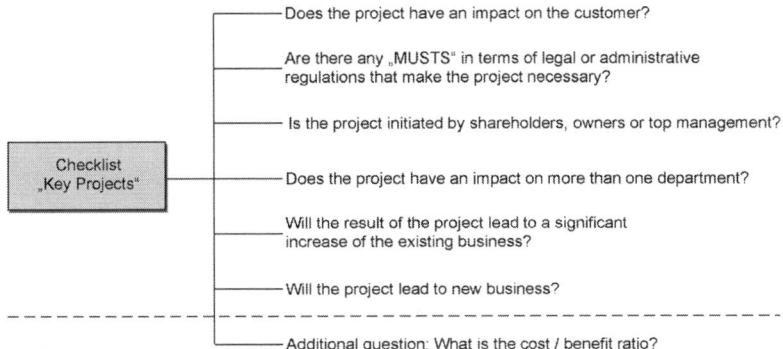

Figure 10: Key Project Checklist

Distinguishing between key projects and "normal" projects is essential for the successful implementation of GPM. Only the key projects are of fundamental significance for the company management. A single department project can fail occasionally. But the failure of a key project can put the entire company at risk.

The Preference Matrix
an effective Prioritization Aid

The preference matrix is an effective aid, both for prioritizing projects and for determining core competencies from a list of presumed capabilities. It is also excellent for putting goals in a weighted sequence. And of course, its use is not limited to work – weekend activities, private investments, or the use of the chronically too short vacation time can be ranked. Here a word to the wise – use of the preference matrix in private life should be coordinated with your significant other to avoid annoying them ("We're not at the office now!").

The preference matrix is based on the principle of pairwise comparison and is not a new instrument, but one that is very simple and effective. The method leads to a structured ranking and also encourages discussion.

Greater Objectivity

Let us view the item "prioritizing company goals" as an example. All company goals considered important should be collected and then compared with one another, one at a time.

In the discussion with your colleagues, a variety of goals are often mentioned and a broad spectrum is developed that also includes goals that you would never have considered.

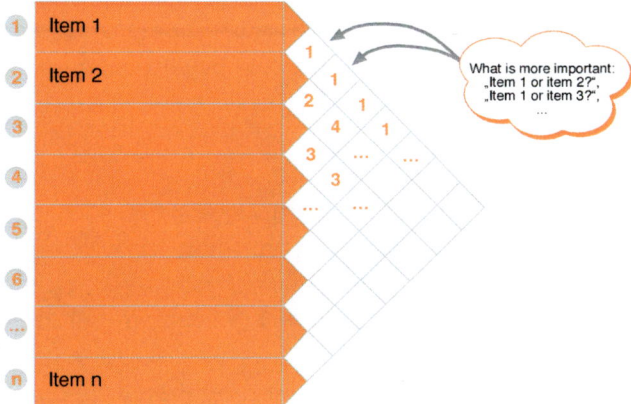

Figure 11: Preference Matrix

The core question associated with prioritization is: "What is more important, goal A or goal B?" This pairwise comparison leads to a ranking list that shows clear priorities. The condition for the success of such a comparison is that the criteria for deciding are clarified in advance. The question "What is more important?" cannot be seen in isolation, as it requires a selection of criteria on the basis of which it can be more or less objectively decided for each comparison why A is more important than B. For example, is one goal more important than another if it results in savings? Is a sales-enhancing goal more important because market shares need to be achieved? The questions as to the criteria for deciding must be answered before, but at the latest during prioritization. Of course, department goals must be oriented to company goals, company goals to shareholder expectations, etc.

Three important steps mark the way to using this instrument:

Brainstorming

In the first step, the possible goals are compiled by brainstorming (of course, mind mapping is also an alternative) and then transferred to a preference matrix. Make sure that the list does not exceed fifteen items, or it will be too difficult to prioritize. Initial gross priorities can be set during this (discussion) phase.

Pairwise Comparison

In the second step, each criterion is compared with every other one. "What do you consider more important, A or B?" It is important here that you – and the group as well – specify a clear preference for each of the elements. The answer "equally important" is thus not possible. When explaining a priority, a discussion often arises. If this prioritization is done in a group, you should agree in advance how a final decision is to be reached. Then a voting method must be found. The easiest method is a simple majority. If one goal is clearly preferable to another goal, it is entered into the matrix.

Analysis and Consequences

In the third step, the number of mentions is determined by counting the entries. Then the goals are ranked according to frequency. The goal mentioned most often is given the highest priority. A presentation of the results in percentages also provides clues as to how unambiguous they were. Is there one clear top goal or are several goals ranked very closely? If two goals are mentioned equally often, the goal that was chosen in the direct comparison is considered more important.

The preference matrix is a very efficient method, which unfortunately is not used often enough in daily routine. The effectiveness of the preference matrix is not limited to the pairwise comparison. Rather, it is the structured process of brainstorming, setting criteria, and deciding on and deriving consequences that ensures that clarity of goals ensues. Try this process at the next opportunity. You will be surprised by the results.

Clean Up Your Prices
Pricing As a Growth Catalyst

by Martin Gierse

The definition of the assortment, that is, the combination of products offered optimized as much as possible for customers, is one of the classic core activities of business. For each and every product, commercial businesses must decide what price their customers are willing to pay and how much they can sell at what price. In an extreme case, the number of individual prices would correspond to the number of products offered.

Such a situation could be incomprehensible and unsatisfactory for customers, and it is almost impossible to compare the varying perceptions of product quality by price. There must be a logical system to structure prices in a manner that is acceptable to customers.

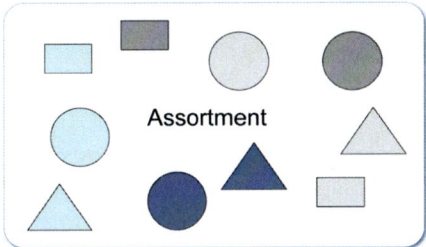

Figure 12: Assortment

Product Groups

To structure the great variety of products offered, the assortment usually consists of several different product groups. A product group consists of all products that can be grouped together on the basis of a common feature. The greatest advantage is orientation for the customer, but also the management of individual product groups, e.g. in purchasing, for positioning, creating offers, in product management. What effect does this have on prices? If products are grouped together, can this be easily transferred to prices?

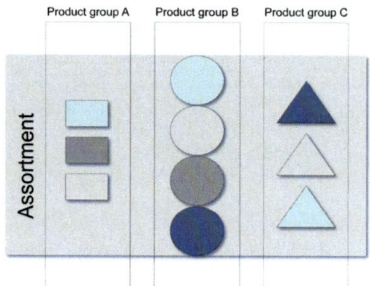

Figure 13: Product Groups

Depth and Breadth of the Assortment

Two important parameters determine the assortment – its depth and its breadth. The depth of an assortment depends on the number of variations of a product within a product group. The breadth of an assortment ensures that the offer of various product groups is as comprehensive as possible.

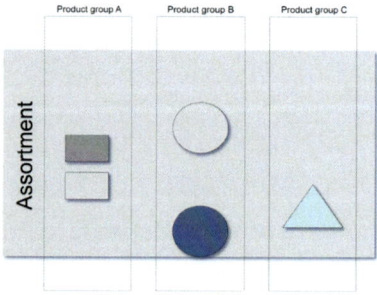

Figure 14: Depth of the Assortment

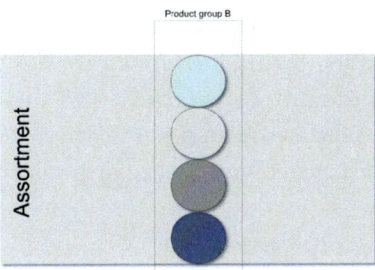

Figure 15: Breadth of the Assortment

Price Categories

This digression into assortment policy creates a basic understanding and leads us now to the topic of price categories. If we focus on the prices of individual products within a product group, we see that they should follow logic similar to the division of products (into product groups). Product groups create orientation within an assortment. Price categories create orientation within a product group. The common feature of a price category is the price or the price range.

What are Price Categories for?

If companies market a very broad assortment, the product groups include a very extensive offer of products of varying qualities and prices.

Price categories divide the prices of products of a product group into various price ranges. The price range is limited by two prices, the so-called "price points". How great the range is, i.e. the difference between the upper and lower price points should be decided on a case-to-case basis. The price ranges offered may be always the same or they may be different. The important thing is that all products in a comparable price range are grouped together. Groups are formed into which the various products can be categorized.

Price categories should be homogeneous in themselves and heterogeneous among themselves, for customers often link the price category with the quality of an article and the price category can thus make it easier for a customer to make a decision between alternative products. Products with a similar price (and quality) are in the same price category; products with different price (and quality) are in different price categories.

This makes it possible to address different customer demands or even different groups of customers. The customer is given room for decision-making and he can choose which products he wants to buy in which price categories. There will be customers, for example, who buy only in the high price categories across all product groups, and customers who combine from different categories.

In order to ensure this selection, attention must be paid that different price categories are offered for all product groups. If one product group contains only expensive, high-quality products, another only medium and low-priced items, the company misses out on sales opportunities and confuses the customer, who, especially if he is interested in the entire product range, wants to decide on his own which price category to make his selection from. The question remains as to how many price categories a company divides its product groups (and thus total product range) into.

Number of Price Categories

The number of price categories is theoretically unlimited, but complexity increases with an increasing number of price categories. If, for example, a retail company offers a deep product range, that is a large number of variations in the product groups, it can be assumed that the number of price categories will also increase. In any case, the number of price categories should be the same or at least similar across all the product groups of a line so as to offer the customer orientation in the entire product line and present a consistent price structure. Commercial companies often offer their customers three price categories –high (top prices), mid, and lower price category (initial price category). Optimally, the customer should have the choice among three discernible products and product qualities across all product groups.

Price Points

Price points are prices that occur frequently within a price category and act as an anchor. The price category starts from the price points and extends from there. Price points should not be confused with prices for key products. Key products are a special feature of the product range policy and are uniquely perceived by customers. Customers also particularly note the prices for key products. Some companies use the prices for key products to present an especially reasonably priced image. In this case, you must go along with the competition. The prices for the own key products must be adjusted to those of the competition. The opposite of key products are side products: products and prices that are given little notice by customers. They offer an opportunity to increase profits by raising sales prices at a relatively low risk. If this is taken too far and sales sink disproportionately, the price can be lowered again. However, care should be taken here to ensure that you do not get the reputation as a price gouger.

Extremes

Sometimes an assortment may include extremely expensive or extremely cheap articles. A decision must be made as to how to deal with these extremes – either the extremes are adjusted to fit the price category, resulting in an extension of the price limits, or they are treated as isolated exceptions.

Conclusion

In assortments with a large number of products, there will be an equal number of individual prices depending on the pricing strategy. The complicated jungle of prices bears the risk of confusing the customer. Do your customers and yourself a favor by arranging the assortment in product groups and price categories. Higher price categories address a clientele that is interested in quality and is willing to pay the corresponding prices. The margins may be higher here than for other price categories. Products that distinguish a company in the higher price categories and may be considered luxury goods offer the greatest opportunity for a high trade margin.

You can use the prices of your products in the lower price categories to give yourself a competitively priced image, for example through directed advertising. Give your customers the opportunity to decide on their own which price category they are interested in and use price categories to address classes of customers that you do not normally reach.

PART II

LEADERSHIP AND
CHANGE MANAGEMENT

The Leader As a Role Model
Nine Factors for Successful Leadership

The question arises again and again as to what are the attributes of a successful leader. As always, there is no pat answer. However, our experience reveals the following nine factors for successful leadership that indicate a broad range of personality characteristics at the personal level which are routinely required of an leader.

Radiate Self Confidence and Energy

It is not necessary to be a charismatic leader to be a successful executive, but without the dedication, without the executive being committed to the task, leadership will not function. People want to follow a person who is convinced that he is doing the right thing and champions this with the necessary energy. Whether this is equivalent to charisma is a good question and depends on the definition of charisma. The important thing is that the leader infuses his ideas, concepts, and visions with the proper amount of emotion so that the employees can see that he the issues seriously.

To radiate self-confidence, certainty, and energy, it is naturally necessary to possess this self-confidence. It is not helpful for a leader to attempt to convey self-confidence to employees when this is not the case. The first step is to build up self-confidence and only then will the employees notice that the leader is serious.

Self Control

Self control is an essential aspect of a leader's personality that allows him to act prudently even in critical situations. This does not mean that a leader should not react emotionally at times. On the contrary – the leader's emotional involvement strengthens the leadership process considerably. But it means that a leader should always keep on top of things in critical phases, when things can get muddled. The leader thus takes on the role of a pilot who has to guide a ship safely into the harbor when seas are rough.

Be Consistent, Predictable, Firm, and Fair

These personality traits mean that the leader does only what he says he will and is clear and unambiguous about it. In addition, it is commendable if the leader demands no more of others than what he is also willing to do himself. And vice versa, the leader must deal with employees' expectations that he comply with his own demands, figuratively speaking, with respect to his own tasks. For example, it is absolutely indispensable that a leader who demands honesty and other socially desired values also incorporates them in himself. If a leader demands that employees keep promises and are reliable and that they give prompt notice if there are any possible conflicts with due dates, the leader must also do the same or risk causing employees to give up. Moreover, strong leaders act consistently in comparable situations and do not stumble from one situation to the next.

Be Methodical and Transparent

Leaders who convey self-assurance because they show employees clearly that they have a plan that, in an ideal situation, the employees can help with, enjoy a high level of trust. The methodical and transparent handling of procedures, figures, data, and facts is an instrument that is essential for including employees in the work of the division and giving them responsibility. A leader who proceeds methodically and deals with information in a transparent manner will always be more successful than a leader who keeps a lid on information. This requires a certain amount of stature, for giving information always entails giving up some power.

See the Big Picture and the Details

Only if you see the whole picture can you lead a team to the goal. "It is better to see the big picture more or less clearly than see the details perfectly" is a valid premise, but if the overwhelming size of the big picture makes you lose sight of the details, you cannot tell whether a sum of slight deviations might possibly lead to a failure of the entire system. Moreover, details of employees and customers are frequently seen more readily than changes to the overall picture. It is thus important for a leader to see both the big picture and envision a picture of the future as well as being able to keep an eye on details. If a leader determines that he tends more to one side or another, he should regularly consult someone who emphasizes the other aspect.

Challenge and Support

The leader who is capable of both challenging and supporting employees demonstrates balance and shows that he banks on performance and also ensures that employees have room for development. Challenging employees is important so that employees in a position to recognize the expectations made of them. Supporting them is important because the employees should know that the leader is interested in the individual development of every single employee.

Be Customer Oriented

Customer-oriented thinking and acting includes the fundamental personal willingness of a leader to serve. The term 'service' stems from 'serve' and the serving aspect cannot be stressed enough. Success is almost guaranteed for a leader who can direct his own actions and the actions of employees to the needs of internal and external customers. In order to ensure that this is done in a targeted manner, the leader should work with the employees to identify the following – for whom are we providing our services? For the sales department, this is relatively. The answer is "for the customers." But who are the customers for accounting, the personnel department, or controlling? The most important point of view that a leader can convey within his sphere of influence is that all salaries, materials, etc. are paid by the external customers, for if the customers did not demand the company's products and services the whole business with all its employees, buildings, and products would not exist. The basic position of the leader must be driven by the question, "How can we make things better, simpler, faster, easier, cheaper, or more effective for our internal or external customers (for the benefit of all)?"

Create and Maintain Value

The area of value is often underestimated and is frequently equated with material values. But this is more about a normative structure that should be conveyed by the leader and shaped with the aid of employees. A leader who is capable of creating and maintaining values regularly poses himself and his employees the question, "What does the company stand for?" or "What does the department or the division stand for?" Values and the personal relationships among the employees of a division are the emotional glue in the team. The values determine how conflicts are carried out, whether the employees stand by the company and their boss even in times of crisis, the level of dedication, of sick reports, of productivity. A commonly held set of values is an essential component of the company culture.

Be a Role Model and Take Responsibility

A person who is standing still cannot lead. Moving forward is a must for a leader. Moving forward is also what makes a leader a role model. The assumption that no role models are needed today is not sustainable. Employees always orient themselves to their leadership figures, whether they intend to or not. The executive is the role model and his behavior is relayed to employees. In many companies, you can tell as soon as you arrive at the front desk how the company is run. This is expressed in external factors such as how people deal with each other or with customers and in the choice of words and manner of addressing internal and external persons. Being a role model means assuming responsibility. The personal assumption of responsibility by a leader for the actions of the employees is a strength that is in great demand. The leader as a role model is a vital personal challenge.

As a top manager, do not just ask yourself how you personally view the properties, but ask which of your executives are currently at which position. As a senior executive you need to test critically to what extent you have developed the properties described above. How prepared are you to invest in developing them?

Change Management
The Management is the Motor

Giving a company or unit of a company a new strategic orientation means implementing systematic change management. Since change projects pose a fundamental challenge for the employees who are to implement the projects, the reasons for the failure of such projects can often be found here. One cause is the speed with which a change project must be carried out in order to meet the changed requirements of the situation; another cause is the speed with which the conditions that trigger the need for change are themselves changing.

It is the responsibility of the management to ensure the success of a comprehensive strategic change. This makes it all the more important for the leadership to be close enough to the basis to discover what is important for employees and what the opportunities and risks of implementing change are. Two things are obvious – that management cannot implement the project on its own and that success depends first and foremost on winning over associates and only secondarily on the project itself.

Three Core Aspects of Failure

The fact that changes can fail because of the attitudes and behavior of people is due mainly to the following factors:

1. Some employees prefer to deal with an unpleasant, but familiar condition rather than with a possibly more pleasant, but unknown condition.
2. The management does not always include by employees in a sufficiently honest and sensitive manner.
3. Managers may intentionally sabotage changes if they feel their

own position is endangered. The loss of one's own position must not necessarily be the main point. It can be enough that the new situation means that the views previously held by the manager are no longer valid. Fear of losing face can threaten to block the change project.

Furthermore, the discrepancy between one's own and others' expectations of one's self and the potentially lower estimate of one's personal skills may give rise to anxiety. But fear is one of the greatest obstacles to the learning and doing that are particularly necessary in times of change.

Hidden Agendas

Hidden agendas are invisible, informal behavior patterns that are frequently known only to those who deal with them directly. Sometimes personal interests are put before the common interest or, quite simply, deeds do not match words due to certain power structures or non-transparent assessment criteria. Management that has distanced itself from the basis will not discover the significant hidden agendas. This requires asking and listening more than speaking. The following question is useful for discovering a hidden agenda: "Let's assume that your best friend applied here and was offered a job. What urgent advice would you give him/her about what to do, not to do, or what he/she needed to know?"

Obstacle or Role Model?

Management in particular can put up high obstacles for change projects. This is sometimes done intentionally by building up distance barriers, or unconsciously by acting out personal vanities and by displaying a disproportionate need for recognition. But even decision-makers who fully back the projects and are dedicated to their company can run into an obstacle if the employees sense that the leadership is not approachable and wants to handle things on its own. While one may not be in a position to deal directly with such unproven, usually unspoken, and often unjustified assumptions, the management can still set the right tone by consistently demonstrating the desired behavior. Patience is needed until the employees see "The boss is serious about this!" but the impact is then even greater. In short, nothing can replace the role model function. This insight completes the circle – the management must make strategic changes and personal aspects play at least as great a role as objective aspects – and probably an even greater one.

The Error of "Motivation" – Do Leaders Really Need to Motivate?

"The foremost task of an executive is to motivate employees." "Motivation is the utmost management goal." "What do executives do to motivate their employees?"

Stop! Here's some news for you: a leader is – are you paying attention? – not responsible for motivating employees. He must create the framework to allow the employees to develop well within the company guidelines so that the employees can create greater value for the company while permanently improving their own (!) level of motivation. Period.

A leader who always gives in to the urge to motivate employees will ultimately fail in this. A person whose goal is to approach employees directly in order to challenge and support them within the bounds of their own and the company's possibilities is on the winning side. Of course this entails encouraging employees, not going around with a glum expression, radiating energy. But "motivating" employees? No. The employees should take care of that themselves.

A Bit of Theory

In order to define the term "motivation" we first have to explain the concept of "motive." Basically, a motive can be described as a reason for a certain behavior. So terms such as need, drive, urge, desire can be synonymous with motive.

In practice, there is rarely a single motive for a certain behavior. Moreover, a person is not always conscious of the motives behind his actions, as actions are often carried out subconsciously. So accessing one's own motives, observing the reasons for one's own actions, and compiling an internal "hit list" of motives are essential phases of self-awareness.

Motivation to do or not to do something arises from a single motive (in rare cases) or from several motives (normally).

In view of the variety of motives that can influence our motivation, there are two major questions:

o Are motives ordered in a hierarchy? Is there an (individual) list of priorities?

o Are motives mutually interdependent on each other?

The answer to these two questions is still disputed. While Maslow postulated the hierarchy of various motives for actions back in 1954, much more complex clarification patterns are used today. Yet Maslow cannot be completely ignored if we observe the world closely. As a reminder, we are showing Maslow's hierarchy of needs pyramid once again, which can be found in this or in similar form in numerous publications.

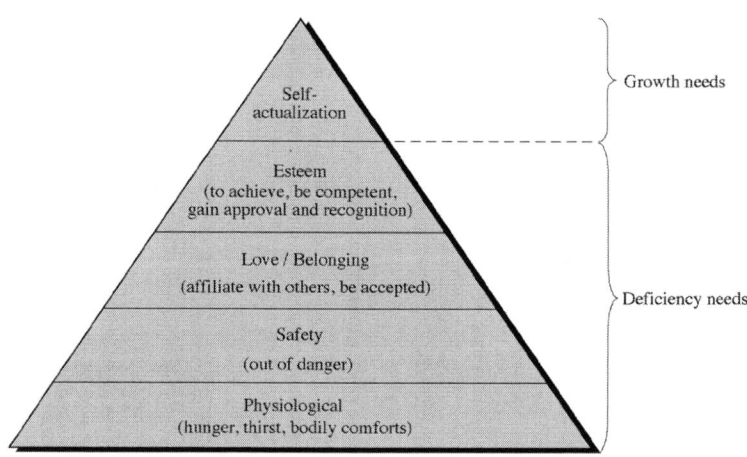

Figure 16: Maslow's Hierarchy of Needs Pyramid

In addition to the so-called "content theory" that assumes the contents of the respective needs/motives, there is a view that assumes a "process theory" of motivation. The Bernoulli principle assumes that the result in which the product of benefit and probability is especially high appears to be desirable. Energy is often invested where the greatest chance of success is anticipated.

What are the possibilities for recognizing motives?

There are different ways of finding out something about motives. Here are four of them:

o   Self-observation
o   Discussions and questions,
o   Shadowing, and
o   Analysis and valuation of the results of behavior

It must be stated that the motives for actions will always be subjective and cannot be made objective. The executive has to learn to live with this vagueness if he wants to develop employees successfully.

Intrinsic and Extrinsic Motivation

We can assume that a certain stimulus that is set meets up with a person's own experience and the sum of his own motives. Such a stimulus is assessed based on personal experiences and gives rise to an action (or alternatively, lack of action). The result of the action can be an internalized result (stimulus: hunger; action: eating; result: hunger satisfied), or an externalized result (stimulus: wanting to win; action: increasing training; result: win the competition). The pattern that arises or the system cycle is identical whether the motivation is intrinsic or extrinsic. The difference stems from which "realm" the stimulus comes from – from the internal realm or the external realm.

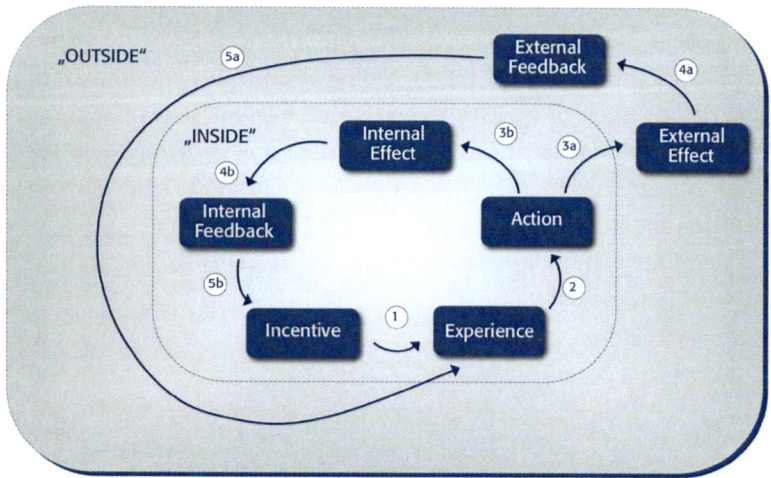

Figure 17:   Intrinsic Motivation

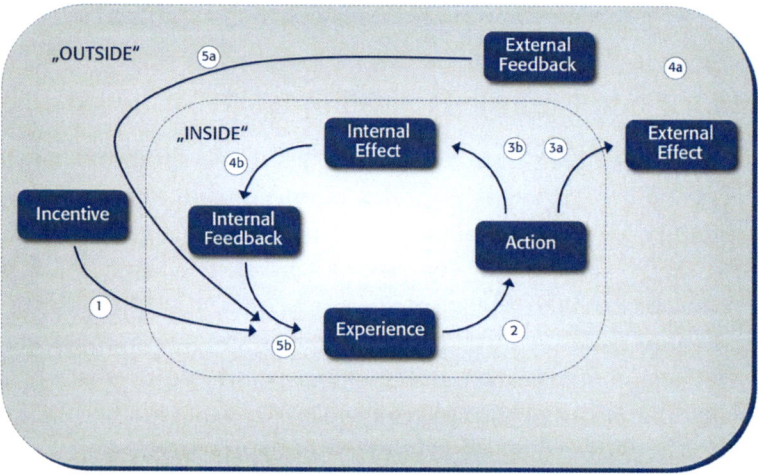

Figure 18: Extrinsic Motivation

50

It is worth exploring the differences between intrinsic and extrinsic motivation when dealing with the issue as to what value internal stimuli and drives have compared with external stimuli. It is safe to assume that internal stimuli are considerably stronger than those one has adopted from the external world or even been forced to adopt (by a leader).

Moreover, these intrinsic motivation factors are more sustainable than extrinsic ones. The goal of the leader must be to find out the intrinsic motivation factors of the employees. At the latest when the daily behavior no longer corresponds to the inner motives, an imbalance arises that costs energy and thus lowers the performance level of the involved person.

One way to increase the degree of intrinsic motivation is to answer the question of meaning. It is only natural that someone who understands the meaning behind an activity and can place the activity in the overall context is considerably more motivated and productive than someone who performs a task in isolation without knowing its purpose because no one ever explained the context to him. Clarifying relationships is a basic leadership task.

Fundamental Issue

The fundamental question is – to what extent it is possible to motivate people extrinsically?

The issue of the possibility of extrinsic motivation has been the subject of scientific studies. The factors that are typically part of extrinsic motivation are always less significant. According to surveys, the so-called motivation factors such as salary, vacation days, status, own car, and other monetary rewards and payments in kind are always of lesser importance than intangible factors – although the importance of externally visible factors in particular should not be underestimated as they boost the ego. But this is only secondarily linked with sustainable motivation.

In a Gallup Survey ("Follow This Path: How the World's Greatest Organization Drive Growth by Unleashing Human Potential", 2002), it is suggested that a company must concentrate on the talents of its employees to be successful. The study made in this work examined the following issues:

o To what extent do the employees know what is expected of them at work?
o Do the employees have the necessary materials and resources to do their jobs properly?
o To what extent do the employees have the opportunity at work to do what they do best?
o To what extent are the employees given real recognition and praise at work?
o To what extent do the supervisors or other persons at the workplace show an interest in the individual employee as a person?
o Does the employee's opinion count?

These factors cannot be measured in monetary terms and there is no reliable parameter for measuring the answers. And yet these questions indicate that there are far more motivation factors than those that can be measured directly and are usually associated with monetary incentives.

Conclusion

Leaders can forget about having to permanently motivate employees. They do not need to do that. Leaders who are capable of recognizing their team's intrinsic motivation factors and can activate the strengths contained there always will be a quantum leap ahead of their average colleagues. Define the playing field, determine the rules of the game, let your employees play according to the rules, and concentrate your efforts on developing the individual performance of every employee according to his or her strengths.

The Leader Personality
Behavior Patterns and Requirements

The question as to typical behavior patterns for leaders is obvious. It would be helpful to have a model, then the long-sought clusters could be formed. Of course, models always have strengths and weaknesses. They can never do justice to the traits of individuals and yet there still seem to be a few patterns. Let us discuss a model, which is simple and easily understandable without oversimplifying things. It relates the leadership style (direct / indirect) to the personality (extrovert / introvert). This yields the following double-axis chart (you know that consultants love those two-dimensional charts ...)

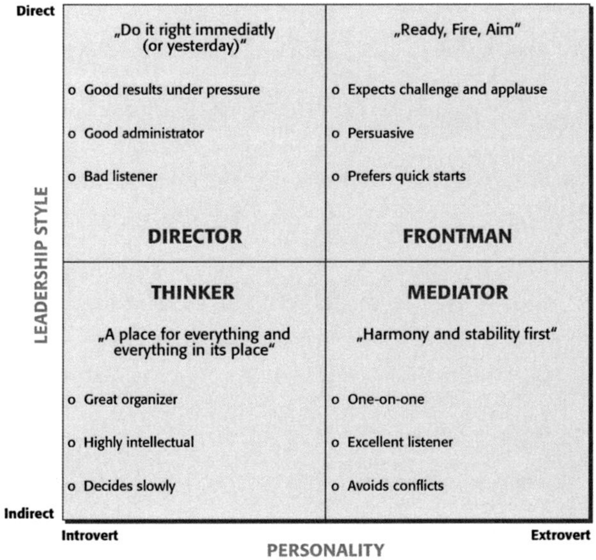

	Direct	
	„Do it right immediatly (or yesterday)"	„Ready, Fire, Aim"
	o Good results under pressure	o Expects challenge and applause
	o Good administrator	o Persuasive
	o Bad listener	o Prefers quick starts
	DIRECTOR	**FRONTMAN**
	THINKER	**MEDIATOR**
	„A place for everything and everything in its place"	„Harmony and stability first"
	o Great organizer	o One-on-one
	o Highly intellectual	o Excellent listener
	o Decides slowly	o Avoids conflicts
	Indirect	

LEADERSHIP STYLE

Introvert   PERSONALITY   Extrovert

Figure 19: Leadership Behavior Pattern

The Director

The director is best described by the slogan "Do it right, and do it immediately (or yesterday)." This leader works best under pressure, and can be described as extremely good at coping with stress. Directors are excellent administrators and are skilled at delegating tasks, but they are not good listeners. They are better are giving orders than at addressing individual needs or interests of the group. Directors send more than they receive, with all the opportunities and risks this behavior entails.

The Frontman

The integrator is marked by his ability to convince others. His motto could be "ready, fire, aim". The integrator can use his great powers of persuasion to influence groups. The integrator needs the group as well, as he expects to meet challenges, experience suspense, and receive accolades in his role as a leader. The integrator tends to make premature decisions, which in turn sometimes forces him to change decisions he has already made. It is then a special challenge to explain these changes to the group.

The Thinker

The thinker's motto is "A place for everything and everything in its place." He is a great planner, organizer, and system thinker. In fact, it is the linkage of these three properties that form his leadership qualities. The thinker understands systems not in linear terms, but in terms of networks as in real life and is capable of grasping these linkages intuitively. He succeeds in making the complex systems and their underlying principles the basis of his planning and organization.

Results are made apparent and the thinker has an excellent basis for handling a project. The thinker is greatly motivated and highly

54

intellectual, so that he rarely needs an external push to increase his level of motivation. The consequences of his planning and organization may be a certain degree of perfectionism, which can then lead to a difficult decision process that is not always to the advantage of the group led by the thinker.

In any case, the above-mentioned features of leadership behavior are only rarely found in their pure form. But something can be gained from viewing them.

The Mediator

The mediator, whose guidelines are harmony, reliability, security, and stability, is an excellent listener who works mainly in one-on-one relationships. His preference for listening conveys openness and the ability to address the needs of individual employees on the one hand, but on the other hand, he does not like to be in the limelight of the leader role and avoids conflicts at any price. He is much more comfortable when promoting individuals than when leading groups.

Requirements

Back to practice. The following seven criteria are sufficient to assess the quality of a top leadership personality. The seven requirements give rise to varying roles that are assumed by the leader. In this way it becomes clear that high demands are made of leaders. The requirements exist irrespective of the company's situation and irrespective of fashions and trends and they complement the previously shown new factors of successful leadership.

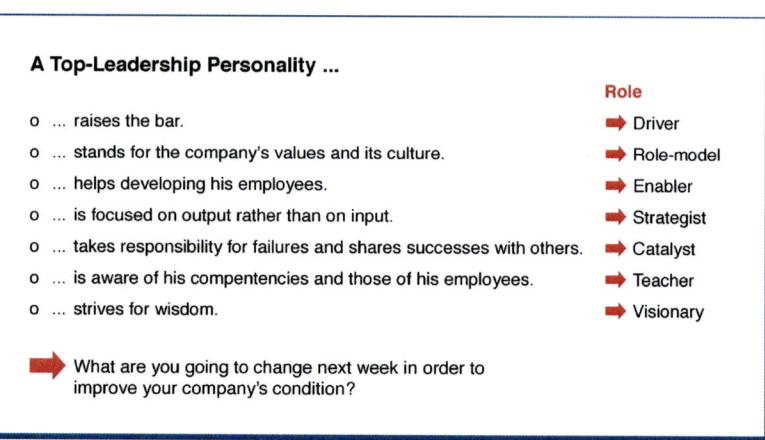

A Top-Leadership Personality ...

		Role
o	... raises the bar.	➡ Driver
o	... stands for the company's values and its culture.	➡ Role-model
o	... helps developing his employees.	➡ Enabler
o	... is focused on output rather than on input.	➡ Strategist
o	... takes responsibility for failures and shares successes with others.	➡ Catalyst
o	... is aware of his compentencies and those of his employees.	➡ Teacher
o	... strives for wisdom.	➡ Visionary

➡ What are you going to change next week in order to improve your company's condition?

Figure 20: Characteristics and Roles of a Top Leader

Situative Leadership
Timing is Everything

What is the leadership style in your company? Is there a consistent leadership style? We get different answers to these questions. Aside from temporary fashions that we do not want to follow up on here because we feel that, at a closer look, management and leadership styles only rarely have any substance (i.e. contribute to the success of a company), we most often meet management by objectives, MBO – of course in varying degrees of strictness and quality. In talks with managers and employees, in addition to the serious suggestions, other "management-by" techniques ("MB techniques") are mentioned, such as the following:

o "Management by Helicopter" (fly low at high speed, kick up a lot of dust, and disappear again),

o "Management by Mushrooms" (keep everyone in the dark, heap a lot of dirt on the employees, and when they pop up their heads, cut them off!)

o "Management by Denim" (the biggest washouts are in the most important spots).

Such sayings are amusing, but at the same time make one stop and think, for they often reveal a bit of frustration – not enough thought has been given to management behavior, there is no apparent management behavior, or it actually is bad. If sayings like this are circulating in the company, you should pay attention.

Management Styles

There is no "perfect style" suitable for all situations. It is usually a combination of various management styles that finally leads to success. In addition, the situation that a leader is managing plays an important role.

An example – a house is on fire, the fire engine arrives. The last thing needed now is a team discussion among the firemen on who takes over what job. This must be clearly specified on the site. The actions and roles must be discussed in advance so that no further discussion is needed. Every action must be perfect. In an emergency, it is better to give clear, well thought-out instructions based on professional and personal experience and to act than to waste time on weighing the pros and cons. I hear some readers say "Sure, that's clear enough if a house is on fire." Beware – a burning house can symbolize a company in financial difficulties.

Good management style in a company is established when the employees know that different situations require different methods. So a good manager has methods stemming from various management styles and has "mastered" the various instruments. Mastery does not come by chance. The principle of predictability must be maintained. The employees will know after some time when which management style seems appropriate and who plays which role in the management process when. Familiarity with many management styles is necessary to achieve this level of virtuosity.

The following chart shows, in addition to the authoritarian, commanding management style, the symbolic, rational, supportive, and generating management styles. Dozens of other management styles can be found in literature in addition to the ones mentioned, with attributes such as patriarchal, charismatic, authoritarian, laissez-faire, or cooperative. There are many overlapping areas in the management styles mentioned below. As always, this is not an attempt at completeness but rather to encourage discussion.

Description	Command	Symbolic	Rational	Transactive	Generative
Characteristic	o Imperialistic o Strategic process is set by the CEO or a small team.	o Orientated on culture o Strategic process based on a mission and on future perspectives	o Analytic o Strategic process based on formal, defined structures and planning systems	o Procedural, orientated on processes o Strategic process based on internal processes and continuous improvement	o Organic, internally established o Strategic process based on internal stakeholders and their initiators
Role of the Executive	o Commander who directs	o Coach who inspires	o Boss who assesses, controls and navigates	o Motivator who empowers permanently	o Sponsor who activates, supports and encourages
Role of the Participants of the Organization	o Soldiers who take and act under orders	o Players who expect a challenge	o Subordinates who follow the system	o Participants who learn and improve permanently	o Entrepreneurs who are encouraged to experiment and to take risks

Figure 21: Overview of Management Styles

The Authoritarian Management Style

We find the authoritarian, commanding management style in mid-sized businesses that are marked by patriarchal management. This style includes command-comply behavior in which the person complying has no significant influence – the management dictates and the employees comply with commands. Due to the predominantly centralistic orientation, this management method is only conditionally suited to bring about jointly supported changes in the organization. It can be observed that a management style such as this is frequently found at the top of the organization and continues down to the various departments. Selected elements of this management style can be helpful for setting management guidelines in the initialization phase of a strategic change project. They serve as a general framework before participative elements of management take effect. Authoritarian management is justified when it is necessary to bring critical, existence-threatening situations under control quickly and there is no time for the participative management process. Authoritarian management requires high input and is not appropriate for allowing employees to participate in the company proceedings. If this kind of management lasts too long, the company runs the risk of attracting mere aiders and abettors instead of decisive, independent employees.

The Symbolic Management Style

The basis of the symbolic management style is a vision that is developed, refined, and sought jointly by the manager and the employees. The role of the leader with a symbolic management style is that of a coach who inspires and motivates.

The role of the members of the organization in a figurative sense is that they view themselves as "players" who are waiting for a challenge and respond to this challenge. While the strategy process in an authoritarian management style stems from the company manager himself or a small team at the most, the origin of the strategy process in the symbolic management style is not oriented towards a person, but is based on a mission and a vision for the future.

The Rational Management Style

The rational management style is very analytical in character. The entire strategy process proceeds from formal, defined structures and planning systems and is anonymized to a certain extent. The role of the manager is the role of the "boss" who evaluates, controls, and directs. In this way, the members of the organization are more like subjects who comply with the system.

Due to the passive, reactive role of employees and the lack of emotionality of the rational management style, it is only conditionally suited to encourage employees or anchor changes in a company. Moreover the fact that it is de-emotionalized means there is a risk of losing sight of the fact that it is generally emotions that lead to action or lack of action. Rational aspects usually cause us only to think, not to act.

The Supportive Management Style

The supportive management style is based on the internal processes of a company. The supportive management is marked by a high degree of enabling support from the manager. The employees are authorized and enabled by the manager to initiate and carry out permanent improvements. The principle of permanent optimization is greatly affected by this management style. The role of the manager is to remove the obstacles from the employee's development, make further development possible, enable him specifically and thus achieve a direct increase in the intrinsic motivation of the employee. The employees learn continuously and constantly improve workflows and procedures.

The Generative Management Style

The generative management style goes the furthest in granting employees freedom and empowering them. Here, the manager plays the role of "enabler," active sponsor, and promoter. The manager is called on to understand the employees as entrepreneurs in the company and give them room to create, to try out new things, even if this means knowingly taking on risks.

Leaders who implement this management style make a contribution to organizational learning, for experiencing the impact of one's own actions can improve the learning process for the organization as a whole. Within the generative management style, the strategy process proceeds from all the internal operators and their initiators. But caution should be exercised when things need to happen quickly.

Summary

Of course, the various types of management behavior are rarely found in their pure form and they can naturally also be combined with the previously mentioned "MB techniques." But where does it say that we cannot manage according to goals or introduce rational elements in a generative management style? It is not necessary that your management style fit a pattern, but it should be appropriate for the given situation and predictable for employees – who ideally should also be able to emulate it. This does not make management easier. But when situative management is mastered, it is a reliable, intangible component of your company's success.

Leadership Catalyst "Coaching"
But What Exactly is "Coaching"?

When a leader has internalized that management is an ongoing process and cannot be conveyed in an initiative, a project, or in a single seminar (and as quickly as possible, please), a significant step in development will have been accomplished. Not infrequently the time comes for a leader when he recognizes that he cannot or does not want to speak with every colleague or especially supervisor about his own development potential. Sometimes the desire for (relatively) objective feedback or the concrete need to reinforce a certain strength or deal appropriately with a known weakness arises and this brings up the issue of coaching. But what exactly is coaching? And what can I as a leader expect from a good coach? The following discussion addresses some of the aspects that we come across again and again when dealing with the topic of coaching.

The Concept of Coaching

There are only a few concepts that are less precisely defined than the term coaching. The range of interpretations of coaching extends from training for employees to a substitute for psychotherapy up to guidance for employees in their daily routine.

There are no limits to the interpretations and the extent of the offers of so-called coaches on the market is truly amazing. The existing objections to professional coaching are due among other things to the fact that business coach is not a certified profession – anyone who feels qualified can call himself coach and there are no qualitative criteria. So the financially lucrative market for coaching is packed with self-styled coaches, amateur psychologists, and unsuccessful business consultants and managers alongside reputable, professional coaches who are qualified to provide genuine, effective coaching and who undergo continual development and targeted training of their skills and know-how. We do not wish to criticize the pitiful efforts to certify the coaching sector (for who decides what a coach can, may, should, and must do, and who then certifies the certifier?), but we would like to point out what is important in coaching in our experience.

Defining the Concept

First, it is important to differentiate between coaching and therapy. Contrary to some people's understanding, business coaching is not therapy and is not a substitute for therapy. For example, if an employee or a manager is suffering from depression, he needs psychotherapy. A good business coach will recognize this quickly and will advise that he seek such therapy. A specialist is needed for this kind of treatment of psychological illness. Amateur psychologists should not attempt it.

Business coaching also has nothing to do with esoteric gimmickry, but is oriented precisely toward goals agreed on jointly with the client, just as a management consultant would do in a project. It is always about bringing the client to a higher performance level with respect to the agreed on goals than before the coaching.

Coaching is usually done one on one and can be just as successful between an employee and an external party as between an employee and a supervisor. Both have advantages and disadvantages, which will be discussed later. Coaching a group is rather rare and not advisable. That should be planned as an internal or external consultancy project. Coaching is an individual relationship.

Business coaching covers two aspects – on the one hand is the material level where results, i.e., improving the impact of actions, building on and optimizing existing strengths are important. The focus is on skills and measurable criteria. Tools can be used for this. On the other hand, there is the aspect of behavior modification.

The coach can influence this aspect only indirectly. He can reflect on it (see "major goals"), but the actual behavior modification will not take place until the client is completely convinced that it is to his advantage.

We view coaching as one aspect of management consulting. I have personally had several coaching mandates and more inquiries are being made. Interestingly enough, almost all these mandates came about during or after successful joint projects. A coach can work successfully with his client if he has acquired the appropriate personality as well as the required methodological competency and project experience from consulting. For this reason, we are very skeptical of pure personality coaches.

Major Goals?

There are a variety of goals of business coaching. The following major goals can generally be seen in practice:
o The own management and leadership competency is improved.
o The personal behavior and effect of personality have been reflected on comprehensively.
o Social competence is increased.
o Concrete new challenges (tasks, roles, etc.) are prepared.
o Support in dealing with difficult interpersonal constellations and in forming challenging change processes is ensured.

Coaching As a Leadership Task

The leader himself will be asked over and over again during the course of his career whether he would act as coach for one (or more then one) employee. Indeed there are many situations in which the leader can function as coach.

When the leader assumes the role of coach (on a case-by-case basis) this must be explicitly discussed with the involved employee or group in advance. This is particularly important, as in a "normal" work environment, the day-to-day business must still be taken care of, projects must be successfully completed, and tasks carried out. So the leader-employee relationship will not be exclusively defined by the coaching process, but a precise differentiation must be made as to when and in what situations coaching is carried out and when the relationship should concentrate on the normal work relationship. Of course, the coachee's limits of confidence in his internal coach are usually reached when he is part of the coach's subjective problem. In addition, this approach is generally limited if there is a risk that aspects of coaching could be exploited by the coach. If an internal coach is to be used, experience shows that it is better to choose a coach who is not associated with the coachee in terms of substance or line of responsibility.

Benefits?

The success of coaching cannot be determined in advance. It emerges within the process as a result of its design. Only during or after completion of coaching does it become apparent whether the process was successful or not. This is frequently a "perceived success" because developing a personality cannot be assessed by measurable criteria. Naturally, this does not relieve the coach and his coachee of their responsibility to define clear goals and parameters that can be used to measure the extent to which these goals are achieved.

Requirements of a Coach

A good coach needs to have a mature personality and have already developed a high level of insight into his own strengths and weaknesses before dealing with the strengths and weaknesses of his coachee. The coach must be able to note in particular the strengths of the coachee, as this is considerably more effective than concentrating on supposed improvement of weaknesses. The coach needs to be able to distance himself emotionally from the issues that he is confronted with. It is indispensable that he knows how to differentiate between observation and evaluation and is able to view situations described to him from his own experience, but integrate this experience into coaching only when this is necessary for the process. It is also vital that the coach is capable of drawing the larger picture of the overall situation in order to offer the client perspectives and visions and to move from the level of detail to the surface. Finally, a good coach offers a balance between "asking questions" and "giving advice."

Basic Precondition for Coaching

The most important condition for successful coaching is that the coachee himself realizes that coaching is useful for him. The likelihood that imposing coaching on someone will be successful is always unlikely if not downright improbable. Only if the coachee is convinced that it would be worth it to at least begin coaching and then to see how things go is there a chance for successful coaching.

It is also essential that the issue of confidentiality be discussed if the company allows an employee to undergo coaching. Are the conversations between the coach and coachee confidential or does the employer expect to be updated on relevant topics and progress? The cards must be put on the table so that it is clear from the start how much confidentiality is ensured.

If you then find a coach who fulfills the requirements listed above and is not just a "yes man," if he is someone who is open to critical discussions and offers opposition in order to demonstrate possible counterarguments to his own position, and if he is a coach with consultancy experience who is a critical sparring partner whose goal is to support you as a coachee professionally and personally and who you like, then you will have the basis for successful coaching.

Teams in Change Processes
Beware of Alibi-Teams

A crucial key for enabling employees to deal with changes in the company is forming teams such as is indispensable in particular for project work. It is essential with respect to the term "team" to note that by no means does every group of people working together form a team. Although teams are becoming increasingly significant in practice due to the performance of real teams, real teams are still not the rule in projects by any means. In simple terms, a team is a small group of persons with complementary skills who work together for a limited time with mutual responsibility for achieving a common goal.

Teams are still a great management hype – but not every problem needs to be solved by a team. For certain tasks, loosely formed working groups can be more efficient than teams formed especially for this purpose. It should also be noted that project teams must always be in contact with the company and may never operate in isolation from the organization, as they would then run the risk of developing their own agenda and not working to serve the needs of the company.

Teamwork can take various forms. The highest level that can be achieved is the high-performance team. A high-performance team differs from a normal team in that all members of a high-performance team are aware that the failure of one member of the team results in the failure of the whole team. The individual members of a high-performance team are thus especially motivated to ensure the success of the other team members. Real high-performance teams are rare and often produce spectacular results.

We find high-performance teams typically in sports, for example in swimming relay. Furthermore we find high-performance teams in emergency situations, like an emergency surgery. In businessit is really hard to observe those kind of teams, but if you had the opportunity to see one at work, or moreover, to be part of it, you'll never forget this experience.

The least effective work form is an alibi team. Alibi teams call themselves a team, but are actually only a more or less randomly formed group whose members work next to each other, not with each other, and without any mutual responsibility for each other. Try to identify alibi teams in your company and stop doing whatever they do. Alibi teams cost you time and money and most often everything they claim to achieve can be achieved easier and with more a effective usage of resources.

Now, where is the bridge between a "normal" working group and a potential team? Whether this bridge is crossed is not always clear. It depends mainly on the parties involved and on the task as well as on the influence of the leader.

When a real team is formed to carry out a task, the combination of common work products, personal development, and results of performance in conjunction with commitment, skills, and responsibility can become increasingly effective.

It is notable that real teams can rarely be found at the top of the company. This is possibly because the management often consists of high-profile managers with successful careers who are convinced of their own methods and do not necessarily wish to adopt the approaches used by their colleagues. This is too bad, because even at the top, some tasks should be done using a more team-oreitned approach rather than using a "silo-approach."

However, not every problem needs to be solved by a team. Alibi teams pose a danger to the change process and "teams at the top" are not usual, nor are they likely to be found. And – the process of forming a team must be done with care. In project work, the sequence "forming, storming, norming, performing" must be implemented and followed through methodically if the team is supposed to unleash its full potential.

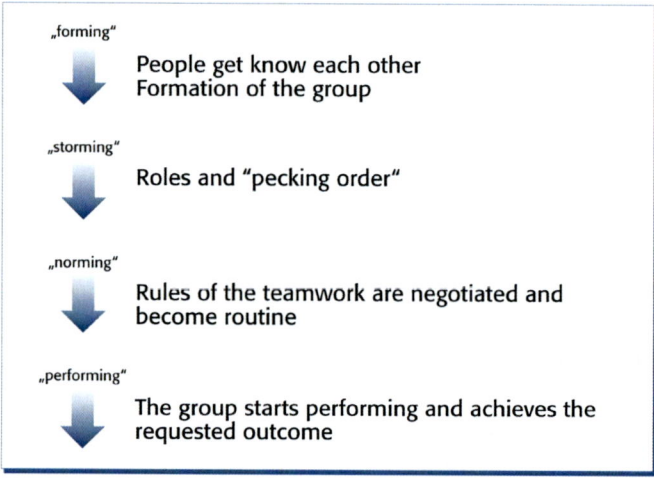

Figure 22: The Sequence of Forming a Team

Don't be Afraid of Conflicts
The 10 Golden Rules

by Susanne Fiss-Quelle

Conflicts are unavoidable in private and in business life. Those who attempt to avoid them automatically find themselves with new conflicts. It is better to be prepared, for handling conflicts is easier than you think if you have mastered a few rules. The following are the 10 golden rules for dealing with conflicts.

1. Be True to Yourself.

Be clear with yourself: what unfulfilled expectations caused your anger? Speak your mind. Don't make any concessions or poor compromises for the sake of peace. State your needs and what is really important to you. For example – I need reliability about deadlines or feedback within 24 hours.

2. View Conflicts Positively.

In every conflict there is not only the risk of injury, but a chance for development as well. What is the positive aspect of your conflict? In addition, many things are not as they appear at first Distinguish between behavior and intention. The "obnoxious" driver on the freeway could be someone driving his pregnant wife to the hospital.

3. Prepare for Your Discussion of the Conflict.

What do you hope to achieve, what is your goal? What do you need? Example – I need short reaction times to give the customer binding information. Do not try to change the other person. Seek the source of your happiness and unhappiness in yourself. What can you change on your own? Have you formulated your expectations clearly and understandably? Acknowledge behavior that you (honestly) value in your counterpart. This creates an open atmosphere for discussion. When preparing for the conflict discussion, jot down ten positive characteristics of your counterpart.

4. Ensure a Suitable Atmosphere.

Speak in private and without disturbances (no phone calls, turn off cell phones).

Take enough time. A quick talk between meetings will no do justice to the issue. Agree on communication rules if needed. For example – listen to each other and allow the other to say what he has to say; keep communication above the belt, etc.

5. Address Conflicts As Quickly As Possible.

Immediately address what is bothering you. If you are emotional about it, let off steam beforehand, sleep on it, or at least take a walk around the block. Then address the conflict openly in a calm voice. Criticize the concrete behavior that you find inappropriate, not the person as a whole. Negative criticism requires a positive counter-suggestion. What behavior do you wish to see? If possible, address foreseeable conflicts in advance.

6. Send "I" Messages and be As Concrete As Possible.

What causes your anger? Name the inappropriate behavior as concretely as possible so that it is tangible for your counterpart. The other party thus gets the chance to change something concretely (if he wants to). Avoid generalizations and other killer phrases such as "You always come too late.", "You never answer my e-mails.", "Things were never like that." Stick to the concrete example and formulate your expectations clearly.

7. Argue Constructively.

Stay objective. Maintain respect for one another and avoid personal attacks. Listen to your counterpart and let him speak.

8. Strive for a Win-Win Solution.

Keep an eye on your needs and your goal. But remain "flexible." What need is hidden behind your counterpart's behavior? There are always more possibilities than you think to reach a solution that is good for both sides. It is important to pay attention to your feelings. Do not agree to anything unless you are comfortable with it. Write down the results of your talk. Putting it in writing makes it more real.

9. Be Consistent.

It sometimes happens that someone just does not keep agreements reached. In case of doubt, terminate cooperation. Look for someone who supports and strengthens you. An experienced mediator or coach can help you solve conflicts constructively.

10. Change Your Perspective.

Have you ever seen the earth from the perspective of a space shuttle? From way up there it looks like a beautiful pearl and you can hardly imagine that there could be serious conflicts there. Do not argue about small things, only for things that really count.

PART III

ORGANIZATION AND PROCESSES

Structure Follows Processes and the Earth is Flat

by Holger Kampshoff and Guido Quelle

The organizational structure must be aligned to the copmany's processes – we hear this demand repeatedly and we support it. However, the organization says "yes sir!" and nods obediently before returning to business as usual, resisting change and without giving it a second thought. Process oriented? Not a chance.

What answer do you get when you ask a person what he does in his company? "I work in the purchasing department (or controlling department, sales department, etc.)". People usually think inside the organogram box. The organogram provides security; it shows how far you have made it up the ladder. How do we measure the personal success of a person in the company? Frequently by the budget he is responsible for measured in dollars, euros, pounds, or whatever, by the size of his office measured in square feet, or by the height of his chair and whether it has armrests, the number of windows in the office, or the number of employees under him. None of this says a lot about orientation to processes, let alone to the results of one's own actions.

A company lives from the profits on sales to customers. Sales are generated in a chain of value-creating processes. Except in the case of personal services, customers are not usually interested in who provides the services, but only in what emerges for him at the end of the value chain. Consequently, the whole company should support this value chain and thus serve the customer.

We differentiate between internal and external customers. Each – internal and external customers – should have only one contact person who addresses their respective problems. The key question is – how can the processes and then the organization be configured so that internal and external customers do indeed have one contact person who provides them value at a reasonable internal outlay?

The Craft

One answer to this question ensues less from ingenious concepts than from proper systematic procedure. But first a rough orientation grid must be created, in which the main processes ("core processes") for providing services are defined. The methodology of the process landscape has proven itself well in numerous industry, commerce, and service provider companies irrespective of their size, including implementation in a major hospital. It forms the basis for the detail work that follows and stems from the conviction that value-creating processes should be interconnected and be visible at a glance. Beginning with the needs and demands of customers and the market, the procedures are developed from a bird's eye view that can reflect these customer needs. The process chains that arise are then complemented by advance services, the starting conditions, and subdivided into main processes. Each main process requires advance services and concretely measurable (quantitative & qualitative) results.

As an example, the following figure illustrates a generalized process landscape for the three core processes of wholesale businesses (sales, definition of product line/purchasing, and operations).

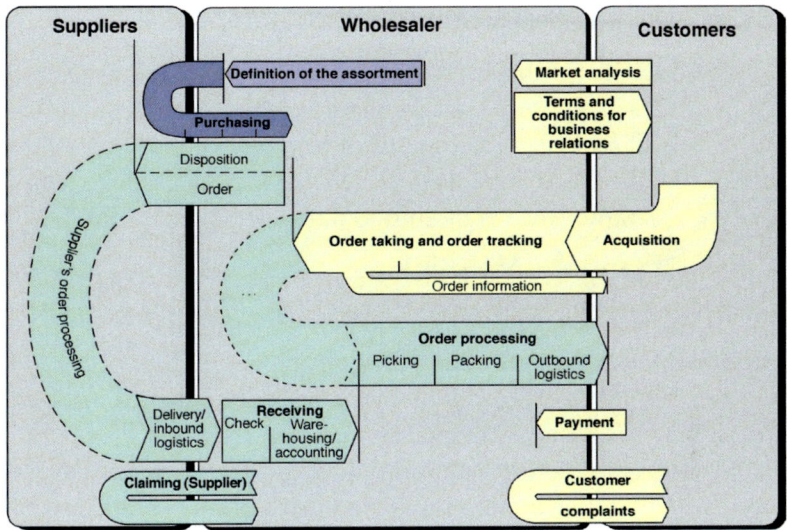

Figure 23: Process Landscape for Wholesale Business

Once there is a consensus on which process configuration is useful from the company's standpoint, responsible parties for the main processes are identified, named, and appointed. These responsible parties ensure that the agreed results are achieved in the operational business.

In the second stage, the main processes are detailed in partial processes and the procedures are worked out in such detail that the pathway to the individual results of the main procedures strived for is described in a precise, transparent manner. This ensures that only those tasks arise that contribute directly or indirectly to providing services. The model used to detail the individual processes is the following:

What Kind of Organization is Needed?

The question of the appropriate organization is not asked until all processes at this top level are firmly set. To do this, the process landscape demonstrates the significant processes and their critical interfaces. The management can derive the required functions from these to guarantee the results and to manage the organization.

Cross-Organizational Thinking

The orientation of an organization to performance processes promotes task-related thinking beyond the boundaries of the individual employee's organizational unit, for a process quite often cuts across several divisions or departments. But when the process result is the major goal, divisional boundaries in the organization can be overcome by achieving the same goal using a process. Process-oriented organization is thus more likely to arise through hard work than through ingenious ideas. The right method does not ensure complete success, but partial success at least.

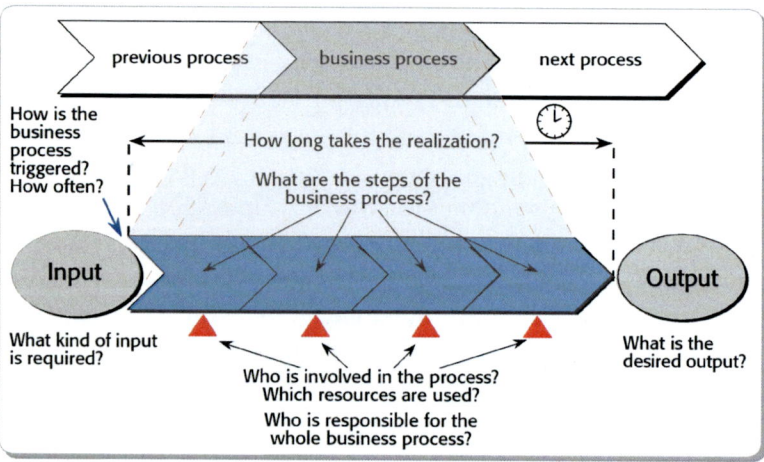

Figure 24: Zooming into a Business Process

Your Company Needs to Grow But Does it Already Know that?

The decision as to the correct time to initiate a growth phase is not so easy. On the one hand, companies should not start implementing a new growth phase too late, but on the other hand it is important to create the proper organizational and processual conditions to allow growth to take place. So there is a thin line to tread between actively waiting and being overeager. It is obvious that to manage a profitable, growing company you need the proper methods and orientation. The challenge of increasing sales and raising profits disproportionately is so great that you can't get very far with "business as usual." So the core question is how a company can generate profitable sales and how the organization can support this. How can the organization be structured, how can managers manage things to ensure that the entire organization is capable of recognizing growth opportunities and generating profitable growth?

It is unrealistic to demand that all company units be ready for growth before a growth project can be initiated. However, our experience has shown that there are a few central organizational locations that must be well prepared before growth projects and the associated extra work they entail should be started. Let's have a look at some details of a random company.

Controlling

The clout and effectiveness of the controlling department becomes apparent in the growth issue. Controllers are often derided as "bean counters" as they are always pointing fingers and attempting to keep costs down. But what happens when the controlling department is supposed to find out whether growth opportunities are promising or not?

What are the instruments that controlling has at its disposal to identify and validate areas of the future? Does controlling cooperate with the other departments or just "control" instead of directing? What is the prevailing mentality in the controlling department? Are the employees famous or infamous for only finding errors or do they take a proactive role in terms of a company radar? What are the feelings towards controlling in the rest the company? Is the department avoided or actively consulted? Is it a service department whose reliability and leadership are praised or is it an administration department with a great deal of power that tells the chairman of the board what he wants to hear and is always wiser after the fact?

Research and Development

In the research and development processes, preparing for growth means processually mapping the interfaces at the edges of the department. What information goes into the research and development department and what information goes out from the department into other divisions of the company? We frequently see that this is unclear, which leads to a lack of information on the actual state of development or to the analysis of old data. Neither situation is satisfactory nor desirable and thus in these processes, it is essential to work at the interfaces to the adjacent divisions in the company.

It is obvious that the interface between R&D and sales in particular plays an essential role, as the mutual provision of information is a major concern with respect to the future market presence of the company.

The competence of the research and development department cannot be assessed on the basis of ongoing projects, but only on the basis of success that has been achieved. A research and development department that only produces ideas that are not marketable in the end cannot get away with arguing that it cannot be known beforehand whether an idea will actually mature to the marketing stage or not. The decisive thing is that the management gives the research and development department clear instructions to use the market and anticipate potential market developments.

How are the individual projects within the R&D department interconnected? Does the right hand know what the left hand is doing? What commercial support is the research and development department given? What ensures that the research and development projects are in line with the company strategy or at least with market segment strategy? How is project organization in the R&D department? Are projects generally carried on longer than anticipated or are results of research and stages of development reported on time? How does management ensure that the R&D department has the necessary market competence?

Marketing

The people in the marketing department are often dismissed as "creative eccentrics." While this judgment is harsh, it is not without grounds, for in the past, marketing concepts were developed in some companies without any understanding of the subject at all. Additional services are added to existing services, unfortunately without this being appreciated by the customer. The results are more work, greater complexity, higher costs, no appreciable benefit for the customer, and no profit.

How process-oriented is your marketing department? Is effective market research carried out in a transparent, easily comprehensible manner? What is the quality of the concepts in your marketing department? Are the concepts sufficiently precise, reliable, and supported by marketing research? How well is the marketing department organized? Are there regular meetings in which insights are shared and transferred to projects in an organized manner? Or is the marketing department something like a pool where everyone can work as he sees fit? How can the marketing manager guarantee that the marketing department utilizes the sales data available in the company and networks with the R&D department?

What controlling instruments are used regularly in marketing?

Sales

"We are responsible for the company's sales and are thus especially important!" – That's right. But we should not lose sight of profits. Selling by giving discounts and low prices is not really difficult and does not lead to profitable growth. So this raises the question as to how sales management ensures that the sales department is sufficiently informed on how to present the products in their best light and how the individual sales employees ensure that the benefit that is created for the customer is known and features prominently in the sales talk. What the company wants is not important, but what the customer wants – and even more important, what he needs – is crucial. Certainly not every customer wish has to be fulfilled, but the customer must at least perceive some tangible benefit so that he will want to buy something.

Of course, the entire sales department does not need to be optimized to initiate a growth project. But is must be ensured that the sales department can handle its job. It is also important that information gathered from your customers (or your customers' customers) is compiled accurately, completely, and as promptly as possible in order to be provided just as accurately, completely, and promptly to the company, where conclusions are drawn and steps decided on. The sales department is the part of your company with a direct market presence and cannot escape its responsibility to convey market information directly to the company. Only when this task is completed can a growth project be based firmly on reliable information.

How does the leadership of the sales department ensure that the sales employees sell at a profit? How is information from the market systematically conveyed to the company and its departments? How does the company acquire information regarding competition? Is there an orderly process for sales research or is the research done more or less randomly? How are customers integrated into market activities? What levels of service can customers have access to, how can additional incentives to purchase be created? Is there a profitability calculation for providing product and services?

It should be noted that the sales process must be supported by an efficient customer service process that ensures that information on complaints and returns can be analyzed properly.

Dealing with the customer or with the customer's customer is a process that is often given too little attention. The good news − companies that direct sufficient attention to this process will soon notice the benefits.

Human Resources

We know too many personnel departments that concentrate on the (more or less) precise wage and salary calculations and personnel support, in other words, carry out administrative tasks. There are too few personnel departments that are capable of assembling service offers that directly support sales, marketing, and other departments in their work. Having personnel processes in your company that are mainly administrative in nature is not a good starting point for the growth project. To shed the image of an administrator, some personnel departments escape into a flood of seminars that the company offers in a shotgun approach. In our opinion, this is the greatest disaster − administration and holding seminars − these are services that can be outsourced to third parties.

Unfortunately, personnel departments and their responsible parties avoid change like the devil avoids holy water. We are not here to discuss the reasons for this. The fact remains that the personnel department must implement a targeted personnel selection process as well as a targeted talent search and development process that functions independently within the company's guidelines and is flexible enough to meet new demands and challenges. How else can you recruit and develop the right employee for your future growth without too much effort?

A well-structured personnel department thus ensures that the responsible managers of the departments work intensively to build up a career development system in the company suitable for supporting the company's performance goals. The question is – is your personnel department an administration function or a developer of the future?

Logistics and IT

"A promise made is a promise kept," should be the rule if your company wants to be ready for growth. We frequently experience that the sales department makes promises that neither logistics nor the IT department can keep. This results in frustrated customers, loss of market shares, and damage to profitability. Not to mention dents to your reputation that take a long time to iron out.

Are your logistics processes oriented to be flexible when meeting new challenges? Are your contracts with service providers refined to accommodate mutually satisfactory adjustments at any time? Are the processes at the logistics and IT departments linked with each other or are they isolated islands?

Support Processes

Finally it should be mentioned that all support processes on the cost side must be reviewed regularly for their contribution to value, suitability for outsourcing, and benefits.

How does your company ensure that the processes are regularly checked as to these aspects? How do you ensure that the processes are not only cost effective, but performance enhancing as well? How is process performance enhancement ritualized in your company? How is it rewarded?

Management

Be honest – how efficiently do you in management work? How does information move among the individual members of management or the board? How does information move from the management to the organization? Are you constantly busy mediating interdepartmental conflicts or having them mediated? Do you ensure that at least any obvious problems that arise regarding cooperation in management are quickly done away with before growth projects are initiated that require the undivided attention of the organization and that on the other hand, processual deficits are discovered wherever they exist. The old adage "lead by example," applies here as well.

Goals and Rewards

A concluding thought – we often see that companies increasingly tend to link employee salaries with achieving certain goals. Who in the company decides that the goals that are rewarded when they are reached actually support your strategy? Variable pay is meaningful only if employees are paid for achieving goals that ensure the profitable growth of your company.

Every system is oriented to the goals that it has to be oriented to. If the goals achieved by individual employees do not support your goal of profitable growth, they have done you a disservice. For example, how is it possible that a company in which most employees have more than met or at least fulfilled the expectations made of them according to the evaluation system can still lose money? The system is defective. Reward only the desired results.

One Face to the Customer
One For All or All for Everyone?

by Holger Kampshoff

Is it better to deal with the customer in the structure designed by the organization – meaning that the customer addresses his questions directly to the respective department – or should the customer have one specified direct contact person who can solve most customer issues directly – occasionally by consulting an internal expert? This question is often the subject of controversy.

In a large pharmaceutical wholesale company with several branches we supported a project with the goal of implementing a call center for customer service according to the principle "One face to the customer." The project was planned for a period of six months and included the concept and the implementation phase. The concept was piloted in one of the company's branches.

Initial Situation

Our client's customers had complained that the branch was difficult to reach and simply addressed their questions and problems to any department where the probability of someone answering the phone was greater. The result – the customers often reached the correct departments only after convoluted paths or their problem was not solved. No one at the branch office felt responsible for the customer's questions and problems. In addition, the unexpected high number of random phone calls caused considerable disruptions to the operative workflow at the branch. There was an urgent need for action from the sales and operations aspect.

Project Goals

A dialog with the Chief Sales Officer of the company yielded the following project goals:

1. Measurable increase in productivity through relieving the operative divisions from unplanned customer contacts.
2. Increase in customer satisfaction and customer loyalty through a competent, personal contact person for the customer at the branch.
3. Professionalizing CRM

The project team had to face considerable challenges at four levels:

Level 1: Customer Expectations

The customers accept the model only if they get a highly competent, friendly contact person who can be reached quickly when needed. It was necessary to give the employees personal as well as professional training and to adjust the operating hours of the call center to the needs of the customers. Furthermore, a glossy customer brochure was made for the call center introducing the employees (with photos) and the idea "One face to the customer."

Level 2: Internal Acceptance

The call center has a cross-sectional function and assumes tasks from various departments. In the beginning, the departments had little confidence in the competence of the call center employees. At this stage, our task was to determine whether correct decisions were blocked by personal sensitivities and to remove these blockades.

Level 3: Interests of Call Center Employees

The employees in a call center bear a great deal of responsibility and demands on employees are high in the introductory phase. These challenges were solved by a holistic and well dosed training plan and promoting team formation.

Level 4: Interests of Employee Representatives

Two members of the employee organization were integrated in the project at an early stage. The employee representatives served the project team as a critical sounding board and reported on the results of the projects in their committees, where they were then approved. We made the experience that the early inclusion of the employee representatives often helps to avoid unnecessary irritations that can be aroused by sensitivities.

Summary of the Project

The goals of the project were achieved to the full extent. Beyond the original project goals, the team succeeded in shifting C customers to the call center for support and relieving the sales team appreciably in favor of A and B customers. It also succeeded in providing other branches with a blueprint in which all project results, processes, and concepts were presented in an understandable way. The company thus achieved a project result that could be repeated. At the end of the project, the project team had a taut, realistic time schedule and had recognized the division as a major factor for success according to expertise in the subject matter (project team) and expertise in methods (mandate). And it had achieved tangible results by concentrating on small, quick successes using available resources.

Feedback from the project manager on the client's side, "I have never before seen a project that included both the concept and the implementation."

And the Winner is ...
Sense and Nonsense of Benchmarking

by Holger Kampshoff

When the performance of a company process is to be assessed objectively, companies often turn to benchmarking. The performance of the own system is measured and compared with the benchmark of the sector or the general process benchmark. Everything appears to be simple and logical – it is easy to see at a glance how you stand with respect to the top company or reference in the sector.

Numbers Don't Lie ...

A short digression – let's look at pro football. Won, lost, tied. Divisional playoffs, conference championship, Super Bowl, and at the end of the season it becomes clear who is at the top and who finishes at the bottom of their division. Objective, measurable. The team that has won the most championships in this system is the benchmark. The other teams have to measure up to it. How can this principle be transferred to companies in which sales areas compete with one another? Each deal counts, every dollar in sales pushes you up in the ranking. And the same rules apply to everyone here. At the end of the day the points are added up. "How is the internal competition doing? How good are the colleagues? Tomorrow I'll step on the gas and pass the guy ahead of me." Ranking motivates all those involved and is often cause for concern, for it evaluates performance. The person who stays on top for a long time becomes the reference, is a benchmark for the others.

Inter-Company?

In logistics and supply chain management, comparisons are often made between companies, for example warehouse turnover rate, availability of articles, or return rate. Does the inter-company comparison help us? Are the parameters defined in the same way in all companies? Are the same reference values used everywhere? Suppose we take 98.9 % as the benchmark for the sector for availability of articles. What does this 98.9 % refer to? Does it indicate articles available in the warehouse in a quantity of one or articles to handle an order completely irrespective of its size? Is the parameter defined by the quantity of articles or the value of articles?

If we look for benchmarks for the warehouse turnover rate, for example a branch of a retail store or in a partner/franchise system and compare the warehouse turnover rates with each other, we might ask similar questions about definitions – is the inventory at the POS included in the store inventory? How are movements between the branches handled? Who is credited with the inventory, how are pseudo movements from the warehouse turnover rate handled? How is the benchmark calculated?

Conclusion

The old rule remains – do not trust any statistic that you have not falsified yourself. Simple benchmarks for easily measurable systems certainly contain a great deal of energy to arouse the sportsman's ambition in those involved. The more complex it is and the less we know about the definition of the reference value, the better it appears to be to measure yourself against your own development and push the benchmark for success upwards. It must be decided on a case-to-case basis whether benchmarks are really useful.

PART IV

INNOVATION

A Stable Basis
The Five Pillars of Innovation Culture

The subject of innovation is once again socially acceptable after years of abstinence. Hardly a day goes by without reports of new outstanding "innovative" ideas and honors for innovators and innovative companies. This was not always the case. In the 1990s and after the dotcom crash, press releases, lectures, and articles focused on reorganization and cost cutting. In view of the current global financial situation at the time we went to print in 2009, something similar is feared. Could innovation and reorganization be no more than passing fashions?

By no means. The whole media buzz surrounding the topics of innovation and reorganization should not hide the fact that they are alternating processes, rarely parallel, that must be mastered, but which must generally be run through successively (exceptions are large companies or corporations whose units, brands, and companies work independently of each other and are in different phases). The trick is to translate the approaches to innovation and reorganization into continuous processes that are anchored in the company and are not just a one-off thing, but have been internalized by the company, with guidelines, rules, and recommendations.

Let's concentrate on the innovation. What are the five pillars that form a stable basis for an effective innovation culture?

Separate Reorganization and Innovation

It is essential to create a systematic separation between reorganization and innovation teams. The methods that have been identified as successful in each case are too different, the respective goals are also frequently too different. While reorganization is usually directed toward efficiency and not infrequently to lowering costs, the innovation processes must only secondarily meet certain criteria for efficiency. Innovation is more about following creative approaches and increasing the chance to produce attractive innovations in products, processes, or services.

The methods of reorganization and innovation specialists are frequently different and at the least, mature team management is required to channel the benefits that both methods offer. It is advisable to bring the (re)organization and innovation experts together only when an idea has already matured to a certain extent.

Institutionalize Innovation Culture

Are you aware of any companies whose chairman of the board is also the top research and development boss? Apple is an example of this and Apple has long been known as an innovator – that has long since left the ranks serving fringe groups and whose company has attained unimagined value. Steve Jobs is the CEO and the top research and development head of his company.

The institutionalization of the innovation process is also encouraged if there are designated innovation teams that keep within allocated bounds and are not just randomly formed. Regular meetings on the progress of innovation provide a structure for the innovation process and ensure that research and development stay down to earth, both with respect to the goals set and regarding market acceptance. Coordinating processes between the individual divisions of a company – including research and development – also enhances the significance of the innovation process and is an additional component of a consistent innovation culture.

And it almost goes without saying – of course a strong team is needed that not only is allowed to bring about innovations, but wants to and is capable of doing so as well.

Make an Innovation Plan and Secure a Method

A visible plan complements the innovation method. This plan has to answer the following questions:

o   What innovations are planned for this year?
o   What innovations are we planning for the next 2 or 3 years?
o   When will which innovation be complete?
o   How do we justify the planned innovations?
o   When will which innovation be introduced / be placed on the market?
o   What goals are we pursuing with which innovation?
o   What interfaces in the organization must be observed?
o   What is the implementation project plan for each innovation?
o   Who is responsible for which innovation?

Give Innovations a Mouthpiece

Whether at internal meetings, at conferences, in general meetings, or in dialogs with analysts – companies are often under enormous pressure to succeed. This makes communication about positive results very important and the dialog on possibilities whose results are still vague comes up too short. There is a great risk that at some point one will remember a potential or a presumed promise that could not be kept due to special circumstances. This is not to put a positive spin on the hot air that we always get in the press. But a bit more courage to talk about innovation concepts, to lecture about excellent research and development teams, to follow up and report on the number of product innovations and the successes of these innovations without giving away company secrets is a vital requirement for a good innovation culture.

The innovation culture can also be supported by having leading researchers from the company attend conferences, publish, be in contact with the CEO, etc. The possibilities that professional innovation communication offers – both internally and externally – are numerous.

Acknowledge Successful Innovators

It should be acknowledged, at least internally within the company, when innovations were particularly successful, a product or a service was placed on the market on time, an innovation process went especially well, or a significant market success was achieved. The tribute to individuals and the reward for the team responsible for success play an important role.

Monetary rewards are naturally an adequate possibility, but official recognition in company media sends an important signal in the right direction. In addition, an insight can be acknowledged that has perhaps not led to any innovations, but which ensured that a certain product was not marketed because its lack of success was foreseen.

If these five pillars are resting on a stable foundation in a company, they form the basis for a gradually developing innovation culture. Companies that have not paid particular attention to product or process innovation over the years tend to need longer than companies that have always been big on innovations. However, the former should not use that as an excuse to continue just as before, but it should be an inducement to try something new.

Innovation As a Management Task
Retrieving and Implementing

The question that entrepreneurs, executives, and managers ask is – how can I get an organization that is managed so that it
1. produces conceptual innovations and
2. can also implement innovations?

In our opinion, a clear change in thinking is necessary to answer the above questions. In today's global competition, many companies attempt to base their success on better exploitation of existing resources. They too frequently count on "cash cows" to help them portray the company to shareholders in a better financial light. Innovations, although the word sounds nice, are rarely systematically sought and found.

Creative Eccentrics

This brings us to the crucial point that has to be changed if a company is to actively promote innovations. The often scoffed-at "creative eccentrics" of a company must have a forum that gives them a platform where they can present potential new ideas independently of their current economic feasibility and discuss them with those who specialize in evaluating the economic aspects of a potentially crazy idea.

Here we can move seamlessly to the litany of killer phrases that are cited over and over again as needed: "We can't do that," "That's the way it's always been," "Where did you get that idea?", "That could only come from the XYZ department," or "How long have you worked here, anyway?"

Trend Scouts for Radical Innovations

Be honest – when was the last time you really sat down and listened to one of these "creative eccentrics" or at least thought about the idea that was presented so emotionally and decided to test its economic feasibility and chances for success idea in a further phase?

Some companies demonstrate what needs to be done, whether in information technology or in the world of trends – the concept of a "trend scout" is not uncommon here; in fact trend scouts are actively sought, as people have come to realize that they are by no means just isolated crazies, but can put the company in a position where it can think outside the box and consider ideas that would not normally be among its prime considerations. The important thing is that the trend scouts (you can call this job whatever you think is appropriate for your company) are often in direct contact with the target group and are in a position to make not only linear improvements to products, but to bring about radical innovations that can maneuver the company into a completely new position.

Method?

The basis of goal-directed management is frequently the well-known PDCA cycle. The cycle of plan, do, check, and act as illustrated below is not always easy to manage even in its pure form, and companies differ in how well they master its execution, not to mention review and install an ongoing improvement process.

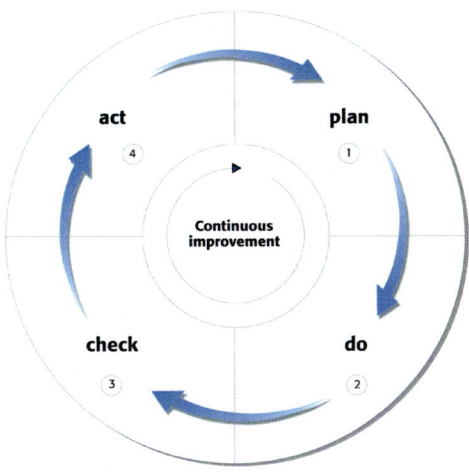

Figure 25: The PDCA Cycle

"Retrieving"

In our opinion, the PDCA cycle as it is classically taught is missing an external trigger, namely retrieve. The differentiation may seem academic at first glance, but in our opinion, retrieving is vital and must be clearly separated from planning, as planning is the systemization of a project and usually offers little room for radical innovations. So what is necessary is to establish the process of retrieving and this is one of the foremost tasks of management. It needs the same attention as the other elements of the PDCA cycle.

The RPDCA Model

Of course retrieving is not everything, therefore we did not just reject the PDCA cycle, but developed it further. Many companies are decidedly good at planning and are capable of translating even complex correlations into excellent plans. If an innovation is then born, it requires perseverance and this is where the first differences between successful and less successful companies appear: successful companies know that implementation requires at least 80 % of the time, in other words, four times as much time as was needed for planning. Consequently, successful companies invest their management principles heavily in implementation and ensure that what have been recognized as good ideas do not get talked to death or worn down in operational business. And naturally, a successful cycle involves reviewing and continual improvement.

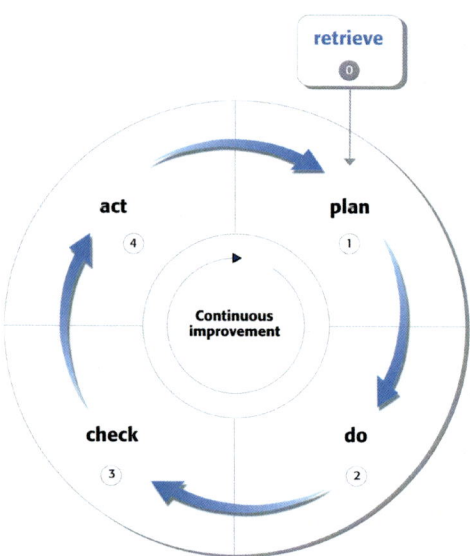

Figure 26: The RPDCA Cycle

Conclusion

The PDCA cycle as it is taught in classic management theory is not sufficient for successful innovation management. It must be supplemented by the element of retrieving, which leads to an RPDCA cycle. For an executive to deal successfully with innovations, there must be, in addition to a successful process concept for retrieving, a great deal of focus on the implementation of the ideas defined as being likely to succeed so that 80 % of the time is spent on implementation and only 20 % on planning. Ideally, innovations are limited to a certain number and the employees are specially trained to deal with innovations. Once this has succeeded, the crucial conditions, at least on the part of management, for a successful innovation process will have been created.

Innovation Sequences
Secure the Foundations

One aspect consists of bringing an innovation into being. The other aspect is the challenge of securing the foundation for growth by a continuous sequence of innovations at the correct time. But when is the correct time for innovations? And how is one prepared for that?

The Life Cycle Curve

We are all familiar with the typical life cycle curve. It is also known as an S-curve and is illustrated below.

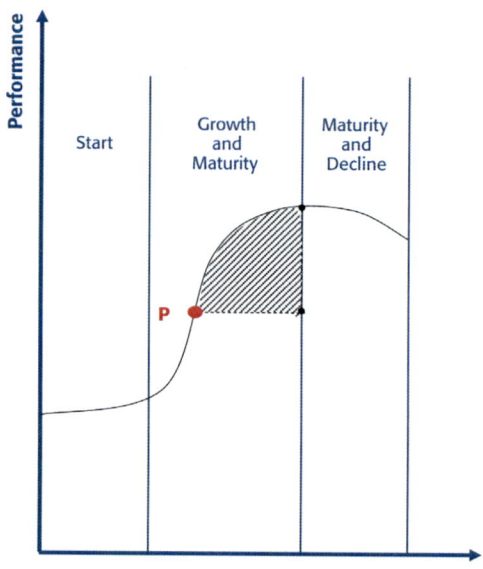

Figure 27: Typical Life Cycle Curve

At the beginning of the life cycle of an innovation, whether for a product or a service, a relatively high investment is usually necessary before an exponential increase yields considerably higher value at a lower investment of time and resources. The steep increase reaches the point of inflection, known to most of us from math – the point of the greatest incline. After this point, growth is still steep, but it no longer increases at the same pace as before. The mature phase that follows is usually followed by the phase where a product or service is discontinued.

The Right Time

There is often the question as to the right time for initiating an innovation. Some are of the opinion that there can never be enough innovation and that a company should introduce as many innovations as possible to the market. Others are of the opinion that there should always be an innovation when a product or service is in the mature phase or at the end of this phase. As usual, the range of possibilities is infinitely large.

Limit Innovations

We believe that it is not at all advisable to introduce as many innovations as possible onto the market, for this can function well only if the entire organization is completely oriented to conceiving, planning, and introducing innovations and it can be ensured that the innovations do not cannibalize the already existing and well functioning products and services. We would just like to mention the saying "haste makes waste."

Not introducing innovations until the end of a product's or service's life cycle can be just as harmful in our opinion, because the right time is frequently passed up and a gap may arise between successful products and the new, innovative products. So there has to be a compromise.

The Point of Inflection

The right time to prepare an innovation is when the point of inflection (P) has been reached on the existing product/service curve.

At this time, when the maximum incline has been reached, when growth is rapidly increasing and further growth rates are clearly apparent, is the optimal time to prepare a new, innovative product or a new, innovative service.

Why So Early?

The reason for this is simple: during the growth phase, the entire organization is oriented towards positioning product "A" with all its advantages for the customer on the market and creating the greatest possible value with the product. When the first successes ensue, when it becomes apparent that the product has been accepted in the market, then the market shares for this product should be expanded and the greatest possible growth rates achieved. If we respect the fact that the introduction of innovation "B" has the same curve as product "A" we must acknowledge that the period between the introduction of "B" and the time it becomes profitable is not negligible. So we must take into consideration that innovation "B" can possibly be financed with profits from innovation "A".

On the other hand, experience shows that the performance of the organization is best when the efforts that are made for the market success are great and lead to corresponding success. This positive momentum must be used to prepare the new, innovative solution "B" and launch it during the mature phase of "A". The correlation between these S-curves is illustrated in the following figure:

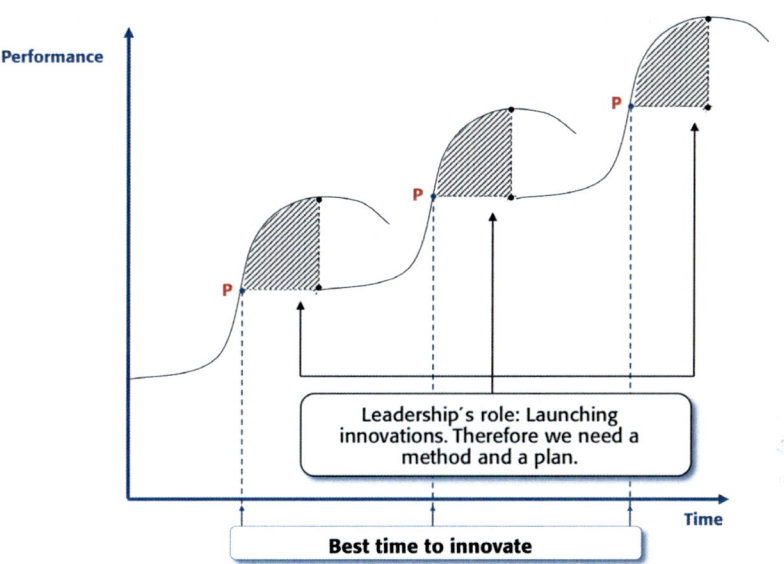

Figure 28: Innovation Sequences

Management Tasks

The task that management faces is to recognize the optimal time for an innovation and to mobilize the employees to create the innovation at the right time. That this is a fine line is obvious to any of us who have already initiated innovations. It is rare that the optimal time for an innovation is found. So dealing intensively with the own products and services becomes all the more important:

o   How many products and services do we currently offer actively?
o   Where are our products and services on the S-curve?
o   What degree of maturity/profits can we expect from our products and services?
o   When will the end of the S-curve be reached?

109

o   Do we want to remove our products/services from the market in the maturing phase or not until their profits start to fall?

All of these are questions that are involved in the management's task of finding the right time for an innovation. The knowledge of the own products and their status within the life cycle is essential for taking innovations to the market using a rifle and not a shotgun approach. In this way, innovations will also be less risky, for thanks to the positive power of the still profitable products, miscalculations and the associated negative effects on profits from an unsuccessful innovation can be cushioned much better than when an innovation is under pressure. Here again – always be one step ahead!

New Things Need Planning
The Well Thought-Out Innovation Concept

Only systematic dealing with innovations brings about the desired success. Too frequently, innovations are brought into the organization as rush jobs and cause problems because a new topic is addressed, employee resources are tied up, explanations from the management become necessary, and the innovation loses steam.

It is better to approach innovations systematically as well. As always, it depends on having the right methods and using them consistently. It is also advisable from our point of view as consultants to implement a method that is already used anyway for planning the business. For this reason, the method of developing a market segment is particularly appropriate. After all, an innovation is nothing more than expanding on, adding to, or (partially) renewing an existing market segment or developing an entirely new market segment. It is thus a valid assumption that an innovation, no matter how general or detailed it may be, can be designed using the principles for developing a market segment. The following is a list of the relevant questions that must be asked when innovations are discussed.

Market Segment

o   What market segment does the innovation arise in?
o   What are the basic parameters of the market segment?
o   What developments can we expect?
o   What are the competing market segments?
o   How do we estimate price elasticity?
o   What obstacles could stand between our offer and our customers?
o   What measures can we take to get rid of these obstacles?

Customers

o In what region can we reach our customers with this innovation?
o Which customers can we reach?
o What are their special characteristics?
o What exact (not just assumed by us, but real) need do we meet with this innovation?
o What wishes does the customer have; what are the actual needs that we need to meet?

Offer

o What is the exact offer that is created by the innovation?
o What is it that now enables us to offer this innovation?
o Is this a fundamentally new service or the expansion of an existing offer?
o What features do we use to meet the precise needs of our customers?
o What is our market message for the innovation?
o What market image will we use to launch this innovation?

Price and Obstacles

o What price do we set as realistic for our innovation?
o What are threshold prices?

Distribution

o What distribution method do we view as promising?
o What organization do we need to take advantage of this distribution method?
o How can the innovation be marketed with existing structures?

Systems and Processes
o What systems and processes do we already have that support our innovation?

o What new processual and systemic developments do we need, conceptual, technical, ... , to translate the innovation as described to the market?
o What part of this do we not need to provide ourselves; what can we outsource to whom?

Organization

o What organizational elements can we implement today to successfully organize the innovation?
o What new organizational elements are needed to adequately manage the described processes?
o What potential organizational collisions can occur if we bring the innovation to the market as planned?

These are just a few of the questions that could be asked when examining an innovation systematically. Of course a definition of the goals, especially of the economic goals, must also be made.

Economic Goals

What economic significance do we assign to innovation? How is the already existing offer strengthened or endangered by the innovation? What investments are we willing to allow for the innovation?

Positioning

Other relevant questions are related to the positioning that is to be strengthened or changed by the innovation. In particular, we need to ask if and where the current position might be strengthened or what changes in positioning might take place and whether the company is willing to make these conscious changes.

Benefit and Effort

The method named leads to a transparency which is not at the basis of all innovations by any means. After the relevant questions have been answered and a positive decision on the conception and realization of the innovation has been made, an innovation project should be planned and systematically anchored in the organization.

You are now asking yourself whether the process described takes time? Yes, it does! And rightly so. After all, a large innovation is not a casual project that can be begun quickly and without thinking it over – often, extensive changes are to be made in the company through innovations, not to mention the impact on the customers.

Our opinion in this respect has been reinforced in recent years – prematurely abandoning existing products and services is just as unwise as not carrying out any innovations in the company. The organization must be in a position to cope with the conception and realization of the innovation and indeed, the innovation itself. The method described thus helps to sound out a supposed innovation for its potential value. In addition, existing strengths of systems and processes are also thoroughly sounded out to be as efficient as possible. Apparent innovations that do not yield any economic benefits (and thus no advantage for the customer) fall through the grid.

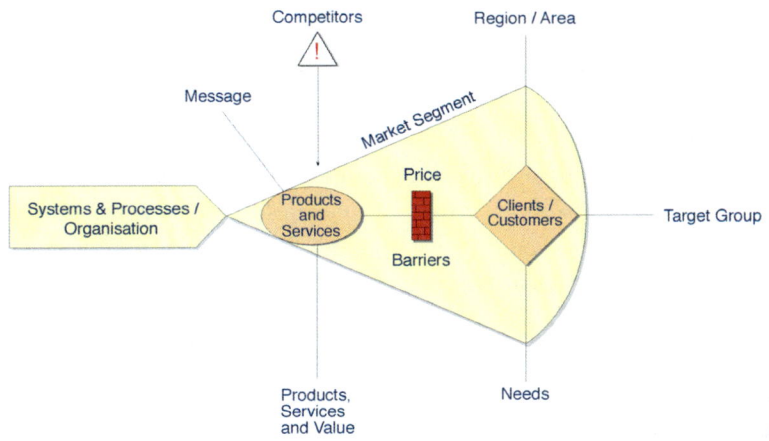

Figure 29: Defining a Market Segment Strategy

During the planning and conception of the innovation project, it also becomes clear what resources are needed and where possible collisions might occur in the company. This raises the issue of priorities – to what extent should innovations already launched be completed or broken off, or innovations that were visualized not be implemented. The method should be a catalyst for bringing about the correct decision based on well-founded knowledge.

Conclusion

A company's well thought-out innovation concept is the basis for continuing success in the future. A strict method helps to create the necessary transparency and consistency in the organization in order to be able to decide whether an innovation seems feasible and is suitable to lead the organization into a new future.

Innovation As a Process
Three Steps to Sustainability

by Holger Kampshoff

What companies spring spontaneously to mind when you think about innovation? Irrespective of your professional background, some companies are named more frequently than others. One company that is almost always mentioned is Apple. Originally a niche supplier, Apple has used its extreme user orientation to gradually gain access to the entertainment electronics sector. The iPod enabled Apple to establish its brand among MP3 players such as "Kleenex" stands for tissues or "Jell-O" for flavored gelatin. At the same time, Apple's music portal "iTunes" built up a completely new sales channel for music.

There are also companies in other sectors such as 3M that come to mind when we think about innovative companies. With 20,000 patents and more than 50,000 products from Post-its to medical technology, 3M must be viewed as a leading innovator. What makes this company so innovative? Is it just the brilliant ideas of colorful personalities? Or is the innovation based on solid hard work?

Innovation According to Drucker

Peter F. Drucker provides a definition of the term "innovation" that includes the processual concept of innovation. *"Systematic innovation therefore consists in the purposeful and organized search for changes, and in the systematic analysis of the opportunities such changes might offer for economic or social innovation".* (Peter F. Drucker, Innovation and Entrepreneurship, Butterworth-Heinemann, 2007, page 31).

In the reality of a company we experience innovation in two ways. One of these is exogenous innovation, that is the innovation coming from outside, in which the company reacts to deficits and carries out changes because of external necessities. However, as we focus on observing innovation as a process, the second form of innovation, namely endogenous innovation, motivated from within, is of more interest. Companies that innovate of their own accord create the framework for innovation. They deal intensively with analyzing customer needs, the market, and changes and develop clear images and procedures to change the company and anticipate potential new developments far in advance.

According to the old master Peter F. Drucker, the innovation process can be classified in three steps that build on each other:

Analyze the Situation

Drucker distinguishes between seven areas that must be analyzed in order to identify approaches for successful innovations.

o The unexpected – the unexpected success, the unexpected failure, the unexpected outside event;
o The incongruity – between reality as it actually is and reality as it is assumed to be or as it 'ought to be';
o Innovation based on process need;
o Changes in industry structure or market structure that catch everyone unawares;
o Demographics (population changes);
o Changes in perception, mood and meaning;
o New knowledge, both scientific and nonscientific. (page 32)

Innovations are not based exclusively on ingenious ideas, but also on a very careful analysis of the seven areas mentioned above, because only knowledge resulting from analysis forms the basis for customers and market-oriented innovations.

Paint a Picture

As Antoine de Saint-Exupéry expressed in his book "The Little Prince," people can be better motivated to change by stirring their aspirations and less by giving them tools or teaching them new methods. Consequently, the images and visions of innovation must be depicted so that they are tangible for third parties. This means that in this second step of the process the ideas that ensue from the analysis must be developed to a clear and multi-faceted image. This should convince the observer emotionally that the only correct thing to do is to achieve the target condition depicted in the image.

This second step of the process is time consuming on the one hand and on the other, is a fundamental precondition for the success of the innovation process. An image that can convince the employees of the necessity for change and trigger euphoria in the employees is the driving power to not only imagine innovations, but to fill them with life as well. If the second step of the process is successfully completed and the employees back the innovation, the third step is a real craft.

Set a Target and Move

In this step, clear and measurable change targets for the organization are derived for the entire organization and formulated as a project. This means that a project framework, a project structure, and a project phase plan are developed. For every partial project, the work packages from the project structure plan that are required to achieve the goals are defined in the classical form "Who does what by when?" In this way, changes in the company reality and thus real growth opportunities for the company arise from good ideas for innovation.

Necessary Overall Conditions

Does a company need a creative thinker to implement innovations successfully? Tim Brown, head of the US agency Ideo, thinks so. He is convinced that a CEO should think like a designer. That means he should have the ability to keep various perspectives in mind and weigh them against each other. "In contrast to a purely technical innovation, it is about empathy and imagination for what people expect. I do not mean only end customers, but all business partners and employees. You have to be able to anticipate needs from all sides and decide what makes sense and what could be successful," says Brown in one of the most important German business magazines (Wirtschaftswoche No. 40 / 2006, page 92 ff.).

If we look again at the market, we will see confirmation of this. Look as Tony Fadell, the inventor of the Apple iPod. He is one of the creative thinkers who recognized a change in the market, developed a vision from it, and took this vision from company to company until Steve Jobs recognized the power of this vision.

Change Culture

If innovations are to be driven forward it is absolutely necessary to build up a culture in the company in which the employees view changes not as a threat but as an opportunity. Here it also becomes clear how important it is to implement innovations as a process and not as a project that is launched when external demands kick in, for in the latter case the employees are always confronted with unsuccessful developments and will tend to connect these unsuccessful developments with themselves as involved parties. This personal link is one of the main reasons that employees hold onto the old and want to show that the unsuccessful development is not a result of their own failures in the past. Once change is positively anchored in the company culture, the employees no longer have a primary personal need to block this process.

Entrepreneurial Support

For Drucker, the entrepreneur is not the person who optimizes and adapts the existing company, but one who is always willing to rediscover his company in its individual facets. This leads to various requirements, for example the selection and management of employees. Entrepreneurs make sure that employees know that that they can make mistakes, that employees feel they are a real part of the company, that employees feel the power of innovation, and that employees feel real responsibility in their divisions. This also includes building up a respective measuring system for innovate work. These are the major conditions for the sustainable introduction of an innovation in a company.

Conclusion

Innovation can be established as a successful process in a company, but what does that mean for the day-to-day business? For one thing, it requires that every entrepreneur and every employee in the company must know his job in his environment in and out, that he deals with it, and that he can think outside the box of routine business to perceive tendencies and changes that affect the own business. We also see how important the marketing department's task of dealing intensively with customer needs and market trends is for the company. Finally, the operative processes should not be accepted as is, but should be regularly reviewed with respect to their objectives in order to recognize divergences and need for change in time and derive all the necessary steps.

"The Sky's the Limit"
When Growth Slows Down

"We will have double digit growth again this year," says the chairman of the board at the annual management conference. "Only consistent growth means progress and standing still means moving backward," he continues. Some 250 pairs of round eyes watch the CEO and you can almost read the minds of some participants that they hear the words but don't believe them. The message is too flat. The sky is the limit? A likely story ...

Growth not only has to be planned, but directed. If you take it for granted that the growth rates of recent years are guaranteed for the future, the limit will be reached quite soon. Many CEOs tend to get caught up in too flat demands for growth, which can be counterproductive especially in uncertain economic times. The question of HOW to grow too frequently remains unanswered. In addition, many CEOs lack the sensitivity to accept that partial – or even total – growth can temporarily reach its limits. Why is this so frequently ignored? Because the unthinkable is just not possible.

Innovation As the Key

For a company to develop well it needs continual innovation, a kind of permanent "reinventing" itself and this process needs to be controlled. The need for innovation is concentrated in the following 5 areas:
o Strategy
o Target Group/Needs
o Products/Services
o Processes/Organization
o Management

Innovation in the Area "Strategy"

It is not enough to conduct an annual strategy meeting in which you more or less intensively confirm the work that is already being done. The mark of a successful strategy process is that, with all due appreciation of what has been achieved, it is more closely examined. Has the world around us changed? Have any new competitors penetrated our market segment? What megatrends are there that we need to address? The real test: what megatrends can we set ourselves? Where can we employ evasive maneuvers to be of even more service to our customers? Are we still doing the right thing?

All of these are crucial questions that are asked and must be answered in a well-designed strategy process. If this is done regularly, documented, and added to the company's know-how, an important step will have been taken, for at this point, the WHETHER (should a certain strategic position be taken?) and the WHAT (what is the future object of our market positioning?) are decided.

Innovation in the Area "Target Group/Needs"

The target group and its needs do not necessarily change rapidly, but they change constantly. The fact that there are usually no quick changes in the target group and its needs is the biggest danger, for it means that we often do not perceive any changes that occur in time. The target group must thus be regularly scrutinized and if needed, adjusted by targeted offers. And the needs of the existing target group must be permanently determined and specific innovations must be custom-designed to fit the needs. In our experience, the greatest error that can be observed is that the company defines in isolation and from its own point of view what needs the target group might have. Too rarely is the target group actually included in the development of products and services. To rarely do we see through the eyes of those who will later use the products and services. Out of the ivory tower and into the target group – that should be the motto.

Innovation in the Area "Products/Services"

If you manufacture products – how is your development department doing? If you conduct research – how is your research division doing? If you are a service provider – when did you last adapt your services to the actual needs and market situation? Success takes place when product innovation and service provision innovation is a coordinated process between product developers and market experts. Unfortunately, this linkage is seldom made. We too frequently see that development departments (and research departments as well) isolate themselves and narcissistically attempt to justify their products. Another extreme position is that controlling departments calculate innovative and good products to death. Success takes place when the development and sales departments have their finger on the pulse of the market under the direction of a member of the management and systematically develop their products jointly with the target group. This not only accelerates the overall process, but also ensures that the flop rate sinks.

Of course, a company's product list may not be infinite because this would increase complexity disproportionately. A thorough clearing of the product portfolio should ensure that all involved maintain the overview over the product portfolio. Nothing is worse than when the sales department does not know the own products due to the sheer number.

Innovation in the Area "Processes/Organization"

When was the last time you looked at your performance processes? Do you know at a glance how the major processes – these are exclusively the market-oriented processes – of your company work? Is sufficient transparency guaranteed to ensure high process quality? When did you last examine your company's process landscape thoroughly?

Successful process innovation requires radical thinking. This may mean scrutinizing all support processes for outsourcing capacity, reviewing every administrative action for its contribution to value creation, undertaking complex restructuring to finally adapt the company to its processes, and it may mean that the company looks quite different after the process innovation. Please note – we are not talking about incremental process changes that are undertaken only because the quality management official, the auditing department, the auditor, or anyone else demands them. We are talking about an initial fundamental change of the processes for the benefit of the customer and for more clarity in the organization. So that it is not necessary to permanently bring about radical change, we discuss below a regular process innovation, adapted to the strategy, which leads to your company being in a position to either do the same things with less effort or more things with the same effort.

Innovation in the Area "Management"

The management forms the link to strategy, because here it is ensured that the S-curve of the product and performance life cycle is appropriately controlled. Innovations in the area of management mean that employees must be adapted to the new company situation and are able to develop systems and methods with which it can be determined at which segment of the S-curve the company is for each product or service. If the management succeeds in establishing the corresponding procedures and enabling employees to observe the laws of innovation, it will have done its job well. So new methods and procedures are always needed, although this does not mean that every new management trend has to be followed. It is more important to access a bank of solid methods and procedures which, when combined intelligently, can generate effective management dynamics.

Innovation in the area of management also entails regularly deciding whether the manner in which projects are implemented is still appropriate. And finally, it must also be determined whether the number of projects is appropriate for the company's current level of development. The management aspect thus gains great significance as a component of implementation of the strategy.

Conclusion

"The sky is the limit?" Perhaps. But if that is the case, then certainly not because you do what has always been done. Innovations are the engines of growth and this means also occasionally saying good-bye to favored products, methods, and even to customers.

Innovations in the Food Industry
Think Global, Act Local

by Martin Gierse

A successful pattern of international and global brands was long assumed to be behind the simple principle of thinking globally and acting locally. A company needs to think global and act local to get an edge on the competition. Contrary to the trend of standardized global brands, this slogan has again gained currency today. Consumers increasingly pay attention to a regional aspect of their products and stores. For providers, "think global - act local" means that global thinking should aim for positive effects and local actions should take local needs into account. A balancing act between internationalization and local actions that contains a maze of complexity that can hardly be controlled – one would think. The French Leclerc cooperative has embraced this concept and has been very successful in Europe.

The Leclerc Cooperative

Leclerc has pursued the global approach all across Europe and the market power that entails. The company achieved sales of 32.6 billion euros in 2006. "Think global" means not setting any local boundaries to your thoughts and orienting strategies and plans towards multinational activities. Leclerc consolidated with the REWE Group (Germany), Colruyd (Belgium), CONAD (Italy), and COOP (Switzerland) under the name "COOPERNIC" to a "European Alliance of Independent Trading Companies" to strengthen its position on the national markets through close, cross-border cooperation. So the company does not limit its strategic activities to the French market alone.

Act Local

The independent local retailer of the cooperative can adjust the end consumer prices to the situation of local competition and location and thus set their profit margins on their own. The Leclerc market operators thus have a much greater incentive to deal with the local market situation and can improve their profit situation by implementing the corresponding measures. Those who correctly assess the competition in the local market can win over customers for their products by quickly adjusting their sales prices. What is the economic situation in the area, which products are in particular demand, and at what price? To maximize profits, all these questions should be answered by a Leclerc market director for the company and its customers.

It is not only the sales price that contributes to the profit margin, but purchasing terms as well, and every dealer can negotiate them freely with the supplier. The head office in Paris makes its latest, individual terms available to every branch as a basis for negotiations. The distributor can now decide whether he wants to get favorable purchase terms acting jointly with associates through bundling, or would rather negotiate directly and alone with the local supplier.

Here again, the distributor has to deal with conditions on the local procurement market. The distributor may enhance his product line to satisfy local demand. The company structure with its pronounced local structure prevails even against large, centrally active competitors. The branches of "Hypermarché," which belong to the world's second largest retail chain, Carrefour, are effectively held in check by the dedicated, independent, Leclerc merchants. Market shares are gradually moving from Carrefour to Leclerc.

Conclusion

The strategy at Leclerc is not new, but shows that even in sectors in which the bundling of purchasing power usually ensures a standardized product offering in a market, local customer needs can still be met. These needs are not related to the product offering alone, but to the price as well. They are not related only to the customer; the merchant and the suppliers also profit from this concept and can optimize their situation. All this leads to a high degree of autonomy for Leclerc merchants, to know-how of customers and markets, to entrepreneurial thinking, and thus finally to satisfied customers.

PART V

PROFITABLE GROWTH

Growing Profitably
An Introduction

Growth gives orientation. Setting clear (growth) goals and achieving them is encouraging and also essential for survival. Only few companies get by without clear growth targets – after all, at the end of the year they have to measure where the company will be in comparison with the previous year and to what extent the goals that were set at the beginning of the year have been achieved.

Growth As a Duty?

Nearly all companies have proclaimed growth without defining it clearly. In what dimension do we want to grow? Do we want to sell more products, employ more people, or achieve higher sales volume, so that at the end of the year we can say, "We've grown"? Or is it all just about profits? Our observations tell us that growth is frequently seen as an egocentric, isolated, self-reference parameter. Growth for growth's sake is rarely helpful, and is sometimes even counterproductive. If we define growth as increased sales, that says nothing about the profitability of the company, not even about its market position, because the relevant competitors are completely outside of the picture if we define the growth target in singular terms.

Growth is necessary if a company is to remain successful in the market over the long term. Size advantages, market power, and investment opportunities increase. But does the value of a company also increase? According to an analysis of the 300 largest European companies (published in Harvard Business Manager 2007), the companies who were able to increase sales volume and profits experienced the greatest increase in value. Growth in sales volume of over 15 % led to only a slight yield on shares (3.9) if there was no growth in profits.

A similarly low yield (5.7) ensues if profit growth is high (in this case +15 %) without a corresponding growth in sales volume (see figure).

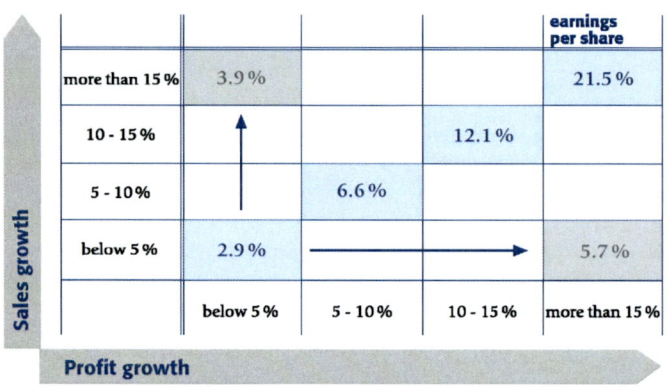

		below 5 %	5 - 10 %	10 - 15 %	earnings per share more than 15 %
Sales growth	more than 15 %	3.9 %			21.5 %
	10 - 15 %			12.1 %	
	5 - 10 %		6.6 %		
	below 5 %	2.9 %			5.7 %

Profit growth

Figure 30: Correlation Between Growth in Sales Volume and Increase in Profits
[Source: Harvard Business Manager (Germany), July 2007]

In our opinion, meaningful growth must also take profitability into consideration. We would even go so far as to say that increasing profitability is more important than increasing sales volume or share of the market. The only exception – strategic considerations that require achieving a certain sales or market share target in the short term. However, this exception is too often used as an excuse for covering up the lack of profitability. Profitable growth thus means:

o The company has increased its sales compared with the previous year.
o The increase in sales is greater than the average growth in the market.

134

o The company has increased its absolute profitability.

o The real test: the company has also increased its profitability relative to sales compared with the previous year.

If the fourth point of the above list is achieved, the company will really have shifted into growth gear. Sales and share of the market are up and profitability, as measured by EBIT or EBITDA is also up. The list of companies that aspire to such profitable growth and also achieve it is significantly shorter than of those companies that would have us believe that they have experienced profitable growth. To determine whether a company has actually grown profitably, it is safer to ask the shareholders, not the company. They will provide much more valid statements.

Five Dimensions

Leading a company to profitable growth is much more difficult than simply allowing it to grow. And of course it makes a significant difference whether a company is guided to profitable growth or whether it needs to be reorganized. There is a time and place for everything. Companies that actually do grow profitably have significant factors in common with respect to the aspects that they emphasize in their internal company development. In our consulting work with growing companies, the following five dimensions proved to be crucial:

o Strategy – What phase of company development are we in? Are our systems and processes already geared for growth or do we have to do our homework first and prepare the company for a growth phase?

o Leadership – How can we harmonize cost awareness, growth of market share, and increased profitability?
o Method – Which method promotes profitable growth? What type of cooperation leads to success?
o Projects – How do growth projects differ from "normal" projects? How can we adapt our projects to stimulate growth?
o Are our processes already lean and quick enough to promote profitable growth? What requirements must new company processes fulfill in order to do this?

Not until the new concept of profitable growth is reflected in the strategy, the leadership, the methods, projects, and processes is a company sufficiently prepared internally to achieve this profitable growth.

Grow or Administer?
The 7 Main Factors Behind a Growth-Stimulating Method

Growth has to be planned, the company has to want it, and the organization must be ready for it. In addition, for profitable growth to ensue, goal-specific methods that are differ significantly different for companies that are aspiring to high growth from companies with traditional development. There are seven main factors:

1. Focus on output
2. Effectiveness before efficiency
3. The best solution is what counts
4. Interdepartmental projects
5. Leadership as a framework
6. Errors show the way
7. More speed than size

Focus on Output

Growth-oriented companies always focus on output instead of input. While traditional companies frequently reward input, effort, activity, workload, efficiency, and behavior according to the saying "If a little is good, a lot is better," growth-oriented companies think in terms of results, not infrequently irrespective of the underlying process. This frequently is a result of the fact that growth-oriented companies are greatly oriented to the needs of their customers – for whom the process of creating a good product or a good service is usually irrelevant, while in traditional companies there is often a high degree of introspection related to improving efficiency.

Effectiveness Before Efficiency

Consequently, growth-oriented companies accept the fact that a result may possibly be brought about in a more unconventional manner if the right result is achieved in this way. Effectiveness, not efficiency has priority. This does not mean that efficiency no longer plays a role for growth-oriented companies, but it is not dealing rapidly with existing problems that take priority, but concentrating efforts on the most effective areas. First comes effectiveness ("doing the right things"), then there comes efficiency ("doing the things right"). This is the guideline. Or better to get the whole more or less right than the details perfect, as Einstein might have said.

The Best Solution is What Counts

Growth-oriented companies focus on finding the best solution, irrespective of whose idea it was. While traditional discussions are frequently marked in that the parties involved want to be right and do everything to prove it, discussions in growth-oriented companies focus on spontaneously questioning favorite positions when a better solution comes up that can offer your client more value. What counts is not being right and satisfying your personal vanity, but finding the right solution for the company, or more precisely, for the client.

Interdepartmental Projects

While optimization is often a priority in traditional companies, growth-oriented companies display a high degree of cooperation in interdepartmental projects. Controversial core issues are discussed here and the respective viewpoints of the different divisions are used to reach a better solution than before. As a side effect, growth-oriented companies benefit from an increase in knowledge from the cooperation of different divisions. In addition, growth-oriented companies purposely reduce their number of projects in order to focus on the main points.

Leadership As a Framework

Growth-oriented companies understand leadership to be a framework that creates the conditions that allow employees to develop. They do not even try to achieve extrinsic motivation, because the employees' motivation must stem from the inside and the leadership needs to create the conditions necessary to promote the development of this intrinsic motivation. While traditional companies frequently view leadership as a directive or regulation, or as reinforcement for motivation in a best-case scenario, growth-oriented companies see leadership as a catalyst.

Errors Show the Way

Of course growth-oriented companies cannot allow unlimited errors and it is a good habit for a person to make a mistake only once. And yet, in growth-oriented companies mistakes are often expressly allowed so that the company and the involved persons can learn from the errors. A "trial and error" philosophy is not established everywhere, but the major difference is that in growth-oriented companies, employees do not need to worry if they have made a mistake. Errors are not dangerous, but rather guideposts that show how a dialog on specific improvements can be conducted.

More Speed Than Size

Growth-oriented companies demonstrate the fact that speed counts more than size by achieving a great impact using few resources. They do not strive mainly for market shares and other traditional features of size; they specifically seek success by focusing resources as much as possible for a greater impact, which then contributes to growth. The traditional striving for market shares is deferred in favor of greater profitability. Growth-oriented companies ensure that everything is oriented toward making or keeping them fast and flexible and they avoid everything to make concessions to speed because of increasing size and increasing political interactions.

Recognizability?

If you observe the company landscape from the standpoint "growth-oriented or traditional?" some of the seven major approaches can already be recognized from without. Sometimes you don't recognize them until you have observed a company more closely. Press releases, publications, or business reports also offer clues as to whether the company's methods are geared to growth or more to optimizing the own organization.

It is obvious that ensuring a growth-oriented environment and appropriate methods is quite a task for management, for here again, they must first demonstrate the desired results.

	Growth-oriented approach	Traditional approach
1.	Results Output Value	Acting Usability Amount
2.	Do the right things Top Down Leaps	Do the things right Bottom Up Steps
3.	Power of the best argument Questioning Holistic view	Power of hierarchy Be right Personal ego
4.	Interdepartmental progress Few number of projects Exponential learning	Departmental focus Large number of projects Linear learning
5.	Leadership as an enabler Intrinsic motivation Create opportunities	Directive leadership Extrinsic motivation Create facts
6.	Learning from errors Trial and error Institutionalized process of improvement	Hide errors Long discussions Situational improvements
7.	Speed Profitability Flexibility	Size Market share Politics

Figure 31: Comparison of Growth-Oriented and Traditional Approaches

Still Reorganizing or Already Growing? Five Questions Before You Start

Admittedly, the title of this article sounds provocative, absolute, pseudo-scientific. And for a good reason, as it is worth thinking a bit before proclaiming in a company that a new "growth strategy" is being implemented. Before a company announces growth, the following five questions have to be answered:

Have You Done Your Homework?

When a growth phase is announced after a phase of reorganization, you need to ask yourself critically the question whether you have already completed all reorganization measures. If this is the case, you can then address the other four questions. If reorganization is not complete, please to not attempt to trim your team for growth – they will not believe it. The preceding reorganization must first be at least 90 % complete.

Regain Terrain or Conquer New Territories?

Do you want to achieve a performance level that your company once occupied and that you had to give up temporarily or do you want to explore new territory? There is a significant difference. For the former, you need a reconquest strategy. For the latter, a strategy for new territory is needed. Do you want to grow incrementally or exponentially? What suppositions are the strategy based on? How do you ensure that the strategy is continued?

Do We Have the Right Team?

A team that has gone through the often-cited valley of tears is not necessarily the right team to open up new horizons. After announcing a growth strategy, you must ensure that you have the right people in the key positions before being surprised by a team that does not know or knows only partially how to approach innovations. Whether with new or existing employees – the main thing is that you are sure that there is enough power at the relevant conception and implementation points.

How Do We Communicate?

This question should actually be answered within the fundamental strategy. Have you given some thought as to how you will communicate the various phases of implementing the strategy? When will you inform your inner circle? Is the next management meeting a good occasion for setting the communication cascade in motion? Who should private talks be held with; when will the presentation be made? Have you considered holding videoconferences so that your message reaches your branches and subsidiaries abroad more rapidly? How do you ensure that the same message is actually conveyed in the entire communication cascade? Is there a motto, a common image, a flyer? There are many correct solutions, but choose one. Make sure that the communication channels are open, for when the information is sent, it's hard to change it.

Are the Measuring Instruments Reliable?

Actually, we should first ask the question "Have we defined the proper measurements of success?" You should be able to see quickly when your growth strategy is successful and when you need to adjust it. What success parameters should express progress? Are these success parameters already known in the company or do you need to define new parameters? Gather up enough courage to define qualitative characteristics!

Of course, sales and market share in conjunction with profitability are suitable parameters for measuring profitable growth, but there are also many qualitative criteria that provide information on the sustainability of your strategy. This begins with the reliability of promises, goes past interdepartmental transparency of activities up to the duration of innovation projects. A headache for the controlling department. Limit yourself to a few real parameters so that you can quickly gain an overview and need not depend on an employee and advisor staff that is programmed to be right.

We have defined and successfully implemented growth strategies with numerous clients. Answering the above questions was never sufficient but was always necessary to be able to proclaim the growth strategy. Strategies never fail from the definition. When they fail, they fail during implementation.

Business As Usual
Is a Growth Project a Normal Project?

Only a few companies deny that they intend to grow in the future – even though a few companies never tire of making the economy, the strong (or alternately weak) exchange rate, world politics, weather, or other circumstances responsible for the fact that this growth never takes place. This makes it all the more remarkable that only a few companies methodically approach the issue of growth and consequently define a project that is suitable for defining the form and contents of growth and ensuring its implementation.

We are approached again and again with the question of what distinguishes a growth project from a conventional project. Are there even any differences? The clear answer is: yes. A project is always a medium that is created to achieve a better condition beginning with the current situation. The question remains whether this better condition has ever been achieved before or whether this better point is a level of achievement that the company has never before attained. This can be explained well using the example of reorganization and I would now like to use two figures by Dr. Alan Weiss (Alan Weiss, The Great Big Book of Process Visuals, p. 47):

The goal of a reorganization project is to reach a level that the company has already once attained. There has been some development in the past that has led to the company losing the original level of performance and allowing a lower performance level to become established. The goal is known; it had already been achieved at one time. Reorganization projects aim at achieving a high performance level again as quickly as possible.

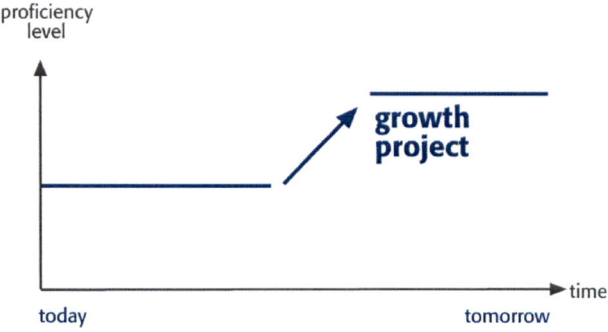

Figure 32: Reorganization Project/Problem Solution (Alan Weiss)

The goal of a growth project is to achieve a performance level that the company has never attained before. It is thus unknown territory and growth projects are thus by nature more experimental than reorganization projects. In addition, growth projects are frequently pending in companies that can afford this growth in terms of time and financial resources. The responsible executives in growth projects are well advised not to listen to well-meaning advice from people who have not yet reached the desired level of performance. Listening is important.

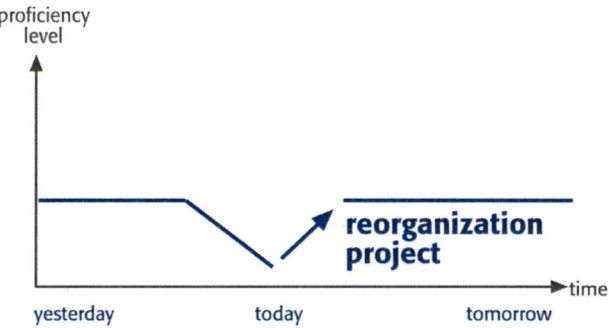

Figure 33: Innovation/Growth (Alan Weiss)

With this in mind, the following are the main characteristics of growth projects:

Responsibility/Project Organization

A growth project is a key project as defined in this book. In a growth project, it is crucial for the management or board of directors to be personally involved. It must be decided on a case-to-case basis whether a member of the board or the management acts as project manager or whether the board or the entire management is the sponsor of the project. If a member of the management does assume the task of project management, it is decisive that this is not just assumed pro forma and is de facto delegated to an employee, but that this leadership is actually operationally executed. It must be considered well whether this step should be taken. But a mandatory condition is that the management actually functions as a sponsor, not only on paper.

Integration of the Organization

One feature of growth projects is that they challenge a large part of the organization, whereby it must be strictly observed that the sales department assumes a major role. Even if this regularly meets with resistance from development and marketing departments, it is urgently necessary to take the later aspects of implementation into consideration promptly; market feedback is received here and must reach the project and the organization. It is absolutely necessary that the project focus on the company's market. In this way, the organization's integration priorities are defined automatically.

Flexibility

It would certainly be a bit of an exaggeration to speak of chaos, but good growth projects are marked by a great deal of flexibility, both in project structure and in work processes. This is due to the fact that a company that initiates a growth project wants to reach a level that it has never previously attained. So it would be stupid to carve all project-relevant aspects in stone from the start and then handle them administratively. But in a growth project it is not only allowed, but even desired to take a high creative share into consideration and this applies expressly to the project configuration as well, which may well change several times during the course of a growth project. While this is fatal in a reorganization project, in a growth project it means that unpredictable changes must be reacted to promptly.

Course

In our view, piloting is absolutely necessary in a growth project to be able to test the reaction to new services and products. While there are differences of opinion here, we at Mandat believe in testing growth opportunities and not trying to score a major coup with a big bang. In this way, undesirable developments have already been discovered in numerous projects and positive developments have been effectively reinforced.

Duration

Growth projects must be designed to be longer term than reorganization projects. In particular, it must be ensured that concept and implementation take place within a project. Of course breaks and phases are useful. But care should be taken that the concept is not separated from the implementation, but that implementation is successfully oriented to conceptual elements and can be safely led.

Interaction

A growth project requires that the parties involved demonstrate a great deal of willingness to communicate with each other. This communication must be institutionalized so that it is not subject to coincidence. The involved parties need to have a great desire to interact, to share even unpleasant details with each other and especially, to ensure that the right information gets to the proper places promptly – and not just in regular project reviews. This is crucial to allow the input of new know-how and not continue to work using old information. Classic instruments for the exchange of information are info boards, project reviews, newsletters, teleconferences, etc.

Explanation of Success

In a growth project it is especially crucial to determine why something worked successfully. Too frequently, the question is asked why something did not work. Growth projects live by distinguishing a pattern for success from accidental success. If success has been achieved, it must be determined whether it is a one-off success stemming from a particular situation or whether this success was achieved due to a well-founded process that can be systematically built on. If a company has mastered this art of distinguishing between situative and systematic success, it will be many steps ahead of its competitors. Deciding whether a success is due to a situation or a well-founded process is difficult and not every company or project team for a growth project makes the effort to systematically determine the pattern for success. If they succeed in this, a significant step toward success will have been made.

Integration into the Company's Project Landscape

In our opinion, companies would be well advised to develop a central growth project or, if there are several growth segments, a growth program. It would be fatal to allow several fragmented projects to run in parallel. Only when the company's resources are bundled toward a growth target can they develop a significant impact. Attention must be paid to which resources are needed from ongoing projects. There is a potential for conflict, for which project manager wants to give up resources, whether in the form of manpower or budget, to another project? The management must be prepared to cushion such conflicting aspects and clear them up immediately. Here as well – unpleasant decisions are better than none at all.

Conclusion

Is a growth project a normal project? No. Many companies already have experience with classical project work and we still see a certain "projectitis," meaning that a company has too many and not too few projects. Only a small number of companies have mastered the art of specifically classifying and creating projects so that they remain controllable and ensure that they support company strategy. A growth project needs – and this is the parallel to a reorganization project – a great deal of attention, must have high, perhaps even highest priority in a company, and a certain amount of tact is required to manage such a project. May the points above be a guideline for you when planning your next growth project.

growth project				
	Status			Status
(1) **Responsibility of directors / Project Organization** Board involved?	✓	(5) **Duration** Concept and implementation in one project?		✓
(2) **Integration of the organization** Sales has a leading role?	✓	(6) **Interaction** Information exchange process?		✓
(3) **Flexibility** Taken care for unpredictable changes?	✓	(7) **Explanation of success** Patterns of success systematically recognized??		✓
(4) **Course** Piloting planned?	✓	(8) **Integration into the company´s project landscape** Only one project with highest priority?		✓

Figure 34: Checklist for a Growth Project

Growing Against the Flow
How to Profit Even in Hard Times

The charts are plunging, some sectors have called on the government for help, and the bailout is growing daily. No one knows exactly how much of the crisis is real and how much is psychological. One thing is certain – even in a crisis there are companies that make a profit. These are companies that are traditionally safe from the ups and downs of the market or even profit from them as well as companies that have taken the proper precautionary measures. Typical sectors that grow even in recessions are the health and senior care sector, book business, pet supplies, do it yourself supplies, and discount grocery stores, to name just a few.

What do successful companies do to be successful even in rough times? The answer is not spectacular and therefore especially interesting:

o   Focus entirely on the target group.
o   Take a critical look at products and services.
o   Adapt the organization to processes.
o   Strengthen sales.
o   Watch the competition closely.
o   Build up cash reserves.
o   Get employees involved.

If this is done systematically, growth opportunities in a crisis will increase dramatically.

Focus Entirely on the Target Group

What currently motivates your target group? Is it still specified sufficiently? Or was the target group allowed to get out of control during good times? Do you and your leadership team determine what potential the target group currently has and how your company can make life easier, better, more comfortable, and more successful for the target group? View the current situation from the standpoint of the target group. Do you really know all the needs of your target group well? In B2B business, the question arises as to what moves your customers' customers. Work together with your team to decide jointly how to clean up your target groups around the edges? Consider also which target group you can now add without diluting your focus.

Take a Critical Look at Products and Services

Which of your products and services have not been changed in more than three years? Have you experienced a drop in sales or noticed that these products have been less profitable? Which products and services have you always wanted to clear out of your offer? Now is the time. Focus on the products and services that actually help your target group, not on those that you think might help an unspecified target group. Provide a solid, reliable service to your existing target group, produce products that the target group can rely on, and do not lower your familiar standards. One mark of successful companies is that they maintain their standards even in times of crisis. Moreover, now is the time to define new products for existing customers and design new products and services for new customers if these new customers do not mean excessively enlarging the target group.

Adapt the Organization to Processes

Now is the time to throw all unnecessary ballast overboard. This should actually have been done earlier, but we cannot undo the past. So explore systematically which useless activities have become established in your company in the past and eliminate these activities immediately. Use the capacities that you free up to improve your core services, seriously consider outsourcing support processes, and adapt the organization to the processes. Too frequently the process organization is built around the persons. This is not only unhelpful, but is highly counterproductive, because breaks in the process lead immediately to decreased efficiency. Orient all processes to the target group and its defined products and services. Ideally, the target group should notice the improvement immediately.

Strengthen Sales

In difficult financial times, many jobs are lost. It is our opinion that now in particular it is essential to retain capable employees and entrust them with value-creating activities. You otherwise run the risk that in the next boom you will have to build up your workforce again. Successful companies ensure that they have powerful resources. This applies especially to sales. If you save in the sales department in difficult financial times – and we mean personnel costs, not material costs – you are cutting off the hand that feeds you. Now it is important to keep the sales department efficient and focus its power on the market. Every opportunity that presents itself to outdo a rival on the market must be grasped. Instead of cutting jobs in the sales department you should now consider whether the department does what it is supposed to do and whether it would not be helpful to even reinforce the sales staff (for example in the back office) in order to retain customers or acquire new ones.

Watch the Competition Closely

How well do you know your competitors? We see companies again and again that claim that competition is not important to them. The fact is that in times when your target group spends less money, it becomes important to turn every weakness of your competitors into your own strength and exploit it. Is your competitor showing a little weakness now in its product line? Wonderful, then take advantage of this with better products. Is your competitor's sales service to your common target group slackening? Great, move into the gap. Your target group will gratefully take notice.

Build Up Cash Reserves

Did you make sure to increase your liquidity substantially during the good financial period? Then you are at an advantage now because you will be able to survive a dry spell when many of your competitors have already given up. A conservative fiscal policy never hurt anyone. If sufficient revenues are used not only to satisfy the owners' needs but also to create liquidity reserves, the necessary means will be there even in a crisis to attempt bigger leaps such as a takeover of a strategically important company. Times like this are ideal for company acquisitions if they turn up from the target group or shareholder point of view. But even if you are not considering a takeover, the cash reserves are a considerable help as you do not need to speak with banks about modifying, extending, or renegotiating loans or the like. The cash reserve offers the necessary peace of mind to proceed without haste.

Get Employees Involved

You cannot do it on your own, but working with a capable team helps you master financial challenges brought on by the external situation. This means that you need to communicate openly what you intend to do. The management must also present a united front. Give your team a perspective, keep in mind particularly that many situations are made more difficult by too much talk and objectively complex situations are worsened by a pessimistic attitude. And the opposite also applies – a positive attitude does not alter the facts directly, but it helps to keep the facts in perspective and see the opportunities that arise from a crisis to find activities that are appropriate for mastering the crisis and achieving initial quick results. Point out that success has already taken place during difficult times in the past. The major steps in the company's development may have been made in especially difficult times.

Get Rid of Boycotters

One thing is very important in these times – if you discover that some employees in your company are constantly criticizing activities, performing poorly, or boycotting behind the scenes, get rid of them. Whatever the cost. You now need employees who offer constructive criticism, not internal troublemakers.

Why Reinvent the Wheel?
Sometimes it Pays to Look to the Past

In general, there is little to learn from the past, for the overall conditions in the present are constantly in a state of flux. We are thus reluctant to say that one should learn from the past and draw conclusions for the future. There are too many factors of influence so that in the end, the lessons from the past are not completely applicable. But sometimes it pays to look to the past, for not everything that was once developed, applied, and implemented has become outdated.

The buzzword "knowledge management" is frequently misused. We want to take a closer look at it under the aspect of using existing knowledge as a basis for multiplying growth.

In order to achieve the goal, reduce effort, avoid doing work twice, and not always having to start similar projects from the beginning again, it is worth delving into the world of project management and project control, for a fortune is spent here because of the lack of methods and procedures and because patterns for success are not documented and are not recognized later. The patterns for success can be found in the following three project phases:

o   Conception
o   Implementation
o   Communication

Phase 1 "Conception"

What happens for an idea for a project in your company? Who is allowed to create projects and has the necessary authority to tap resources (time and money)? How do you ensure that the person who creates a project is informed as to what similar projects have already been carried out in the company with what degree of success or failure?

It is crucial to ensure that access to the company's project data is available as early as in the conception phase. In companies beyond a certain size, work is often done twice. But when this double work is not intentional – and this is almost always the case – the management has to protect the company from investing time and money in projects that have already been worked on, either in another area or in a similar form. Moreover, successful procedures from past projects should at least be considered, even though they cannot always be taken over as is. What worked, what didn't work? What project organization achieved results, what didn't? Under what strategic conditions was the project worked on in the past?

When a potential project manager has access to the answers to the preceding questions, you can be almost certain that the project will be accelerated. Some projects even become obsolete.

Phase 2 "Implementation"

An important question when implementing a project concerns cooperation. What constellations of cooperation – institutional and personal – have proven themselves, what constellations were not as successful? For example, were we especially successful when we involved the IT department at the proper time? When exactly was the "proper" time? What was the experience in involving the controlling department? Was it worth it not to involve the financial and accounting departments in a project? How about the PR experts?

Deriving patterns for success in the cooperation between the company's departments during projects is a good basis for saving a lot more time for future projects.

The use of technology to increase efficiency is very important. Interesting tools are often designed and used in projects that can be if use to the company in other projects as well. It is worth systematically pursuing which technological advance was made in which project, which tool was created in a project, what was the experience with this tool, and for what uses was it more or less suitable. In this way, a toolbox can be created that will be of increasing help in solving certain problems more quickly than in the past.

While the conception phase has many traps that could lead to a project not being as successful as desired, the implementation phase shows the strengths and weaknesses of the concept on the one hand and the reaction from practice to the idea on the other. It is thus necessary to document for projects with care which implementation steps were chosen in order to achieve the desired result as soon and as sustainable as possible. Were there certain traps that became apparent which were avoided in an appropriate way? What uncertainties cropped up in the implementation phase? How did you ensure that future users of the project results viewed the results in a positive light and did not play the "not invented here" card? Are there any traps that were discussed in past projects and which no longer exist because things were handled in a better way? Was a pilot approach useful, or was the project result already fully implemented from the start?

The question of acceptance by the future user of a project depends on his being involved. Here the intelligent configuration of the project team and the associated integration of internal and external customers play an important role

Phase 3 "Communication"

The best project is worth only half as much if nothing is said about its existence and its successes and failures. The greater goal is to have know-how in the company that can be accessed in a directed manner on a case-to-case basis and not just the certainty that this know-how exists somewhere but the search process is too long and is given up.

Too little attention is paid after a project is completed to communicating the achievement systematically, as the next task or even the next project is already at hand. The communication phase thus does not begin only after completion of a project, but when it is configured. Projects have to be announced and cannot be simply "done." The company has to know what it is doing. Simple, understandable reports for various target groups enhance the attention that a project is given.

Here again, patterns for success must be defined and existing success patterns used. When is the ideal time to discuss a project? What existing channels of communication that were proven in the past can be used? Which standard reports proved to be successful in the past, which ones less so? Who must receive information in which form?

Finally, the information should aid the recipient, more than the sender. After a project is completed it is essential to file the results and communicate the information to make it accessible. It is not helpful to submit a comprehensive report that is interesting only for those involved in the project. The know-how should be designed in a way that makes it accessible to the next project team. Unfortunately, due to time and budget constraints, this does not always happen.

In our view, no important project should ever be finished with ensuring the results and the project manager should be discharged only when access to the essential contents and processual know-how of the project is guaranteed.

Conclusion

If a company successfully introduces an "If A, then B" manner of thinking, it has laid an essential foundation for making growth replicable, as benefits can be drawn from successful procedures used in the past. Thinking in patterns can lead to an appreciable acceleration of pace. In addition to top management promoting this idea and the team supporting it, a certain manner of dealing with it critically by reducing it to the essence is necessary to create the need in intended users to use existing information again.

Growth? Yes, But … Not at Any Cost When it is Time to Step on the Brakes

Growth is in, staying in place means moving backwards. Even if the employees and management of companies in crisis are allowed a "growth break," at the first sign of an upturn growth will be at the top of the agenda again. We must become larger, faster, and more profitable. At any cost if necessary. Numerous employees are paid so that a company can grow, sometimes without knowing or understanding what the purpose of growth actually is.

Growth for growth's sake is simply stupid, contradicts common business sense and should not become the company's raison d'être. Eight thoughts on this:

Justify Growth

Why should the company grow? Is growth essential for the company's survival? Is a critical size necessary, or is it about profitability that needs to be maintained? Do market circumstances demand that the company must grow or is pure vanity driving growth? Does the company's size mean greater company value? Or is that not constituted by profitability?

Without justifying growth, a team cannot be convinced to move in the right direction.

Define Growth

Growth must be defined precisely. What is desired, what is not desired or is even prohibited? If a company is sent onto the growth track without the proper guidelines, it is easy to lose focus. Counterproductive projects are started, thinking in terms of market share outweighs thinking in terms of profitability, and complexity increases exponentially. The dialog between shareholders and management on the need for growth and the way growth is achieved must be held very closely to harmonize expectations and results. Without an exact definition of growth, no growth strategy can prosper.

Stop the Nonsense

You especially as the owner of a company don't rely on unrealistic promises. This applies in particular if your management or the management of another company makes promises regarding externally generated growth. The same applies to the management of a company; it must be checked carefully to see whether promises made by the owners when another company was taken over can be kept in the future. We have seen too frequently that companies created such a complex management through random acquisitions – which of course looked promising at first glance, and even perhaps at second glance – that the operational business suffered.

Look things over four, five, or even six times if necessary before making an external acquisition. Stop senseless growth at the onset.

Adapt the System of Incentives

There are still employees in companies – especially in sales – who are rewarded for a certain level of sales or growth in sales, irrespective of whether the sales generated are profitable or not. This needs to be stopped, for producing "bad" sales is not in the company's interest. While sales with below average profitability can be justified to gain a share of the market for the short term (although it remains to be seen how these market shares can later be defended when the prices are raised), care must be taken to ensure that the employees benefit from a company's profit situation, not from its size. Particularly in sales it is helpful when incentive systems are oriented to an order's contribution margin or long-term components such as customer loyalty or customer development are included.

If we emphasize profitability, a share in the yield of a unit of the company, a profit center, or even of the company's performance is more useful for all its weaknesses than a pure share of sales, which can even harm the company.

Information

Growth strategies can be pursued only with informed shareholders, investors, and employees. Without communication there can be no growth. Thus it is crucial that the reasons for and requirements of growth be defined precisely. A lack of communication often leads to such major misunderstandings that even good growth strategies cannot succeed.

Create Predictability and Assessment

If your project managers cannot explain to you how the latest expansion projects have affected the growth strategy decided on, beware. Make sure that growth is predictable by basing it on previously agreed on criteria and ensure also that an assessment is made of the quality of growth projects so that you can determine whether you can continue to press on or need to slow down.

Separate Restructuring and Growth

In a growth strategy, the existence of effective, efficient processes, an effective organization, and goal-oriented leadership are indispensable for success. If the company is in a restructuring phase, it would be senseless to announce excessive growth targets. The sequence is still: first restructure, then grow. The ground has to be prepared before the seeds can be planted. The harvest comes later.

When Do You Need to Brake?

You know that it's time to step on the brakes when one or more of the following occurs:

o You can no longer explain to yourself and others in two sentences the reasons for the growth planned.

o You cannot make a concrete, substantiated statement on the need for growth.

o You have the impression that the number of presumed growth projects is growing disproportionately.

o You discover that employees are rewarded for actions instead of for results.

o Your shareholders, analysts, and investors always want "more" without being able to say why and no one in these groups is willing to discuss the "how" with you.

o You discover that sustainability no longer plays a role in all the discussions.

o You are of the opinion that you as a top manager would do well to put the company on a more stable footing and take the topic of "growth" off the agenda for a while.

The Culture of Growth
A Question of Attitude

Profitable growth needs not only a sophisticated strategy and a clever method embedded in a communication concept for all stakeholders. It also needs a certain attitude and company culture. This company cultural aspect, the "mental mindset," should not be underestimated. If only a few live the culture of profitable growth, it is often too little and leads to some obstacles along the way to the age a growth culture. And finally it will develop a life of its own.

What are the essential elements of the culture of profitable growth in the company?

Start at the Top

Be proactive. This must be management's motto. Delegating and innovating are very important. The management that just administers existing conditions and draws its success from the safety of the past is not a good role model for employees. Many know how to administer, very few how to innovate. The company management is paid to encourage innovation, guide creativity into the proper channels, and take on calculated risks to reap the fruit of the labor in the future. Be consistent when delegating, innovate with a goal in mind, and leave administration to others.

Forget About Being Perfect

Perfection can be a growth killer. If we are not in the life-supporting or life-saving area, perfection is almost never needed and can often only be justified in that it appears to create a secure space for uncertain employees to move in. One of the significant wise sayings that I have retained goes, "Life is about success, not about perfection." After achieving 80 % at the latest, take off running, for otherwise the competition will be faster.

The Right Team

Do you have the right people around you? Are the right people at the right places? Do the working groups support each other or take each other down? To build up a culture of profitable growth, you need a team with a positive attitude. You can't get this from extrinsic motivation, for that is mainly ineffective, unnecessary, and does not bring about results. Look for intrinsically motivated employees.

Address Growth

How does a culture arise if no one talks about its components? If you have decided on profitable growth, discuss it in meetings, in projects, in internal and external communication. Remember – a topic must be discussed seven times before it is understood. Only if a top is addressed often enough can you expect that is will be taken seriously. Direct your attention to projects that lead to profitable growth. Ignore failures unless they are fundamental or you can actually learn something from them. Actively reinforce successful initiatives, encourage innovation, and talk about them.

Generate Responsibility

As a leader you need to specify the WHAT, but delegate the HOW. Even if mistakes are made in the implementation phase, this is generally not as tragic as if you had to take care of every detail. Of course, some leaders will think that they already delegate enough. We believe that there is still a great need to control and that many more tasks could be delegated if they were delegated properly. This is directly involved with eliminating the "I am not responsible" attitude. Define responsibilities clearly and make your expectations known.

Measure and Reward

Make sure that you and your employees continuously measure growth initiatives and their success and systematically reward progress. This implies that failure should not be rewarded. You must distinguish whether a failure was only the lack of success due to a new initiative or a real failure. Reward results and progress, but not isolated activities. Always consider the original intention when you look at success. You will see that your measuring methods will soon be adopted and your system of rewards is appreciated.

Creative Tension

A person whose belly is full moves more slowly. It can't hurt to generate a bit of creative tension to maintain dynamic development. Of course there must be phases when a company has to rest on its laurels. But ideally, this is only sometimes the case, and other areas remain in a state of creative tension. It is no easy task to distinguish and weigh off between honoring achievements and formulating the next objective. We believe that a certain amount of "forward-looking dissatisfaction" is useful in keeping a company on the move and establishing a culture of growth.

Acknowledge

Be sure to acknowledge success sufficiently. This goes for individual successes as well as joint successes. Even if you as part of the management are much farther in your thoughts than your employees, consider what your employees have done to achieve a certain result. Acknowledge success directly. Ensure that lower performers are not acknowledged and are occasionally pushed aside and thus separate the chaff from the wheat. This is also part of the culture of profitable growth.

Growth from Within
Everyone Counts

While teamwork is great and cross-divisional collaboration is important, in the end it is the responsibility of the individual to generate growth in a company. The company and its leaders should and must provide the framework to allow employees to grow and to contribute to the company's growth. Every employee is obligated to create growth within this framework. Only when the employees take responsibility for their growth and when the employees contribute their part for the growth of the company is the company healthy.

Here are five aspects of taking responsibility for growth:

The Myth of Motivation

Employees who wait to be motivated are making a mistake. First, they become dependent on an external "motivator" and thus hand over a significant portion of their own fortune or misfortune to others and secondly, the employees were hired with certain expectations of them, namely, that they assist the company in its success. This may entail a corresponding success for the individual employee, but the company comes first. Wake up! The company still has a right to intrinsic motivation after the employment contract is signed!

For leaders, this means that they should not only make it their duty to motivate employees permanently, but should also concentrate on fulfilling their leadership tasks as well. In concrete terms, this means creating an appropriate framework for the employees and systematically ensuring that employees can develop within this framework. It is not necessary to entertain them, but to attain goals together and thus generate the motivation needed to keep moving another step forwards. If employees are no longer capable of motivating themselves, they should start looking for a new job.

Put Your Ego Last

It is not important to look good, but to contribute to success. With all due respect to the individual, no one should think he is alone in the world. Accept others' successes, set your ego aside on occasion, and ensure that your contribution to success is known, but not overestimated. Continuous success is more sustainable than large one-off successes.

For leaders this means that it is important to allow your own employees to be in the limelight. Success automatically rubs off onto the leader and leads to more success. The person who deserves praise should be the one to get it and not the one who happens to be responsible for that person. A person who is always shouting will not be noticed anymore at some point, and the person standing in the limelight cannot shine brightly.

Develop Yourself Systematically

Continue to work on yourself. Only when you grow yourself can you contribute to your company's growth. Are you bored? Stuck in a rut? It's up to you to find new tasks, attend a seminar, get involved in an exciting new project, or even look for a new company. That would be better for you and your current employer than if you sit around being unproductive (or even counterproductive).

Leaders have to ensure that the employees they are responsible for not only have the opportunity to take further training, but actually do so. Further training should always be a means to an end and must fit into the respective employee's context and his area of responsibility or desired future responsibilities and success should be monitored.

Self Satisfaction

Don't be satisfied with what you have achieved. It can always be a bit better. But you need to distinguish between necessary improvement and perfection. Perfection slows growth down, while a certain creative tension can be a motor for growth.

Leaders need to ensure that their employees can realistically estimate whether the effort-benefit ratio of their work is effective. Introduce a method for measuring which allows you to recognize whether the output achieved can be justified by the input made. Employees often get stuck in the optimization and perfection rut instead of devoting their time to new things. This can cost the economy billions per year.

YOU Count

When a team of climbers crosses a glacier, the strength of every single member of the team is important. If they all rely on an incompetent leader and the strength of the others and are not capable of anticipating the dangers themselves, organizing a rescue from a crevice in the glacier, or estimating the weather correctly, the whole team is lost. It is not just the group that makes them strong, but the interaction of the strengths of competent individuals that brings about success. An experienced team in which every one can really rely on the others and does not just think he can rely on them will get to the peak and back safely. A group of amateurs that assume they are safe because of the sheer size of the group is lost in an emergency.

Leaders would be well advised not to give in automatically to the pressure for more "teams" or "teamwork." Sometimes a working group is preferable to a team. Let us remember that a team works on a specific task for a limited time and the members are mutually responsible for success. When such a team is created, there should be a good reason and competent members. A team is not meant to cover up for weak members who don't do their homework. Distinguish between working group and team and make it clear that in a team as well, each single individual counts.

Conclusion

The presumption that a group will get it right, that leaders have to motivate employees, and that growth will "somehow" happen by itself is not only wrong, but risky. But the good news is – if everyone thinks of his own responsibility to see that growth starts with him, a major element for the company's growth will have been achieved.

List of Figures

PART II

PART III

PART IV

176

PART V

Index